Middle Class Money Shield

Azhar ul Haque Sario

Copyright

First Printing, 2025

Azhar.sario@hotmail.co.uk

ORCID: https://orcid.org/0009-0004-8629-830X
Disclaimer: This book is free from AI use. The cover was designed in Canva.

Contents

Inflation Unveiled—Why the Middle Class Bears the Brunt

Okay, let's ditch the textbook jargon and talk about why it feels like your money is doing a disappearing act. You know that feeling – you're buying the same old things, but the total at the checkout counter keeps creeping up? That's inflation, the slow creep that makes every dollar, pound, or peso feel a bit thinner than it used to. It's not magic, though; it's more like a complex dance between what we want and what's available.

Imagine two sides to this dance floor:

1. The "Everyone Wants It NOW!" Rush (Demand-Pull Inflation)

Picture this: A fantastic new gadget drops, or maybe everyone gets a surprise bit of cash (like those stimulus checks or saved-up lockdown funds). Suddenly, everyone wants to buy things – new cars, holidays, home renovations, you name it. It's like the doors opening on Black Friday, but across the whole economy.

When we all rush to buy more stuff than the factories can make or the shops can stock, sellers notice. They see long queues (real or virtual) and know people are eager. What happens? Prices start to climb. It's not necessarily greedy (though sometimes it is!); it's often just the market reacting to high demand for limited goods. Think back to 2021-2023 – economists saw spending jump while production lines were still sputtering back to life. That imbalance? It pulled prices upward.

2. The "It Just Costs More to Make Stuff" Squeeze (Cost-Push Inflation)

Now, flip the coin. Sometimes, prices rise not because we're all desperate to buy, but because it's simply getting more expensive for businesses to create and deliver the goods and services we rely on. This extra cost often ends up on your receipt. What causes this squeeze?

The Global Traffic Jam: Remember when getting anything shipped felt like a logistical nightmare? When ports were clogged and containers scarce? That chaos made it pricier to get raw materials (like wood for furniture) or essential parts (like computer chips for cars). Those higher shipping and material costs get baked into the final price. Experts looking at global trade saw these tangled supply lines directly pushing up manufacturing costs around the world (like the IMF noted in 2024).

The Energy Jolt: This one hits close to home. When the price of oil and gas skyrockets (thanks to global conflicts, supply decisions, or other big events), it's not just about pain at the pump. Energy powers everything: factories, delivery trucks, farm equipment, the lights in the supermarket, the servers running your favourite apps. Higher energy costs send ripples everywhere, making almost everything more expensive to produce and transport. That 6% global inflation figure experts like the IMF worried about for 2025? Volatile energy prices were a huge part of that story.

The Paycheck Puzzle: Businesses need people. If they have to pay significantly higher wages to find and keep staff in a competitive market, that increases their operating costs. This is a tricky one – are rising wages causing inflation, or just trying to keep up with it? Economists often debate this, but significant wage hikes can add another layer of cost pressure that might nudge prices higher.

From Global Headaches to Your Grocery Bill

These big-picture forces don't just stay in reports; they land right in your shopping cart. That forecast of continued inflation isn't abstract – it means your hard-earned cash buys a little less life, a little less comfort.

Think about a simple loaf of bread. If oil prices jump, the farmer pays more for fuel to harvest the wheat, the trucker pays more to haul it, the baker pays more for gas or electricity to run the ovens, and the supermarket pays more to transport the finished loaves. Add in maybe a higher cost for the plastic bag it comes in because of supply chain snags. Suddenly, that loaf that cost $5 a couple of years ago inching towards $6 isn't just bad luck; it's the direct result of these global cost pressures playing out. While maybe your entire grocery bill didn't jump 20% overnight (as sometimes gets thrown around), specific items certainly saw shocking hikes during recent supply shocks or energy spikes – just look at eggs or cooking oil sometimes!

The Post-Pandemic Perfect Storm:

The years after 2020 were like a giant, real-world experiment. We saw a powerful mix: governments poured money into economies to keep them afloat (fueling that "everyone wants it now" demand), while lockdowns and logistical chaos gummed up the works (creating the "costs more to make" squeeze). Then, geopolitical events threw fuel on the fire, especially with energy prices. What did central banks around the world do? They hit the brakes by raising interest rates, trying to cool down the buying frenzy to fight the rising prices – a clear sign they were reacting to these very forces.

So, while understanding why your wallet feels lighter doesn't magically refill it, it does peel back the curtain. It shows how a shipping container stuck in Shanghai, a conflict far away, or a surge in demand for laptops can ripple through the complex web of the global economy and change the price of your morning coffee. It's a reminder that we're all connected in this intricate economic dance.

The Tightrope Walk: Feeling the Squeeze When Your Paycheck Can't Keep Up

You know that feeling? Like you're pedaling a bike uphill, legs burning, but the summit keeps getting further away? Or maybe it feels like you finally crest the hill, only to find the ground slipping away beneath you? For so many of us navigating the middle ground of life, that's the financial reality right now. It's the quiet hum of anxiety beneath the surface, the feeling that you're working harder than ever, but somehow... treading water, or worse, drifting back.

This isn't just bad luck or a rough month. There's an invisible economic current at play: inflation. It's the sneaky way the price tags on everything – from the milk in your fridge to the roof over your head – creep relentlessly upwards. While prices are sprinting ahead, many of our paychecks are just... jogging. Or maybe strolling. Or perhaps they sat down on a park bench a while back and haven't gotten up yet.

Economists might call it "wage stagnation versus the Consumer Price Index," but let's call it what it feels like: The Squeeze. You're caught in the middle. You earn too much for the safety nets designed for those truly struggling, but you're nowhere near wealthy enough to just shrug off the fact that everything costs more. You're the shock absorbers of the economy, feeling every bump.

Think about that gap – the one where costs are here (point high) and your income is here (point lower). Numbers like "a 3% lag" sound sterile, but translate that into life. That 3% isn't just a statistic; it's:

The brand-name cereal you swap for the generic store brand (again).
The "check engine" light you pretend you don't see because the repair bill feels terrifying.
The family vacation simmering on the back burner for another year.
The retirement account contribution that feels more like a hopeful wish than a solid plan.
The knot in your stomach when you open the electricity bill.

Let's paint a picture. Remember Sarah, the graphic designer renting that downtown apartment? Last year, $1,500 felt tight but doable. This year, the renewal notice reads $1,800. Ouch. That's $300 extra every single month. Her "cost of living raise"? Barely covered her increased health insurance premium. So, where does that $3,600 a year come from? It's scraped together from cancelled streaming subscriptions, fewer dinners out, maybe postponing dental work, or worse, watching her credit card balance tick upwards. She's paying more for the exact same space, just to stay put.

Now, turn the mirror on yourself. Grab a metaphorical (or real!) pen. Jot down what your rent or mortgage was a year or two ago. Now, what is it? How about your average grocery haul? Your gas fill-up? Your childcare bill (if that's part of your world, you know this pain)? Add up those increases. Now, honestly compare that to how much your household income actually increased in the same timeframe.

Did your pay rise enough to cover all that, with maybe a little extra? Or is there a gap? That gap, whether it's big or small, is your personal "inflation trap." It's the erosion of your power, your choices, your breathing room.

It ripples through everything:

The Grocery Gauntlet: What used to be a $150 weekly shop is now pushing $180-$190 for the same basics. That's maybe $1,500-$2,000 extra a year just to eat, potentially wiping out a small raise entirely.

The Commute Cost: That extra $50 or $100 a month filling the tank feels like highway robbery when your salary is stuck in park.

The Childcare Chasm: This is a big one. Costs often skyrocket far faster than average inflation, leaving parents feeling like they're working just to pay for care.

This isn't about statistics; it's about the human cost. It's the constant, low-grade stress of juggling rising bills on an income that feels stuck. It's the feeling that the goalposts for "financial security" keep shifting further downfield. It's the erosion of the ability to save, to dream, to handle the unexpected flat tire or medical bill without tipping into crisis. It's the middle-class tightrope walk, and right now, the winds of inflation are blowing hard.

The Ghost in Your Grocery Cart: How Inflation Steals More Than Just Your Money

We talk about inflation like it's a math problem – percentages on a screen, the rising line on a graph, the extra dollars tacked onto the gas pump receipt. We tally the cost of eggs, the price of milk, the chunk missing from our savings goal. And yes, that sting is real. It pinches, it restricts, it forces calculations we'd rather not make.

But that's just the surface noise. Below the clatter of economic reports, there's a deeper, quieter theft happening. Inflation isn't just picking our pockets; it's a ghost creeping into our homes, whispering anxieties into the dark, fraying the threads that tie us together. It's measured less in shrinking bank balances and more in the weight on our shoulders, the tension across the dinner table, the dreams quietly shelved.

Think of it as a constant, low hum of uncertainty vibrating beneath everyday life. When the cost of everything feels like shifting sand, how can you plant your feet? That worry isn't abstract. It's the knot in your stomach wondering if the paycheck will stretch. It's the mental gymnastics of juggling bills, the exhausting calculus of need versus want versus can't possibly afford. Studies put numbers on it – stress levels soaring, anxiety blooming like a toxic weed (Pew Research, Social Science & Medicine echo this). But the feeling? It's the crowding out of peace, the slow erosion of feeling secure in your own life. Joy feels like a luxury you have to budget for.

And that internal static inevitably leaks outwards, crackling into the spaces between us. Money worries are notorious relationship saboteurs, turning shared finances into a minefield. Suddenly, conversations about budgeting aren't just practical; they're loaded with unspoken fears, flickers of resentment, maybe even blame. Imagine the hushed, tense argument: can we afford that small birthday cake, or does the skyrocketing power bill devour that tiny joy? The love hasn't vanished, but the relentless pressure forces cracks in the foundation (Family studies like Dew & Xiao confirm this pattern).

It echoes in the conversations with our kids, too. How does a parent explain that the soccer league, the art class, the simple joy of participating, is now out of reach? It's not just cancelling an activity; it's the heavy cloak of guilt, the child's confusion, the feeling of letting them down. We see it reflected in community centers reporting lower sign-ups, kids sidelined not by choice, but by cost (a reality often mirrored in local news). We see it in the grocery cart, swapping vibrant, fresh food for cheaper, less nourishing options just to make the numbers work, a trade-off with long-term shadows (Food bank reports chart this grim trend). Postponed check-ups, delayed repairs, cancelled family movie nights – each one a small surrender, a quiet dimming of life's richness.

This personal strain ripples further. When individuals are constantly battling financial headwinds, stressed and depleted, the instinct can be to pull back. Less energy for community gatherings, less capacity to help a neighbor, less involvement in the ties that bind us. The collective weight of individual anxieties can cast a pall over a community, fostering pessimism instead of connection (Research on social capital highlights this link).

So, yes, track the economic indicators. But remember the real story isn't told in decimal points. It's whispered in the sleepless hours. It's felt in the strained silences between loved ones. It's seen in the heartbreaking choices parents make, sacrificing small joys and sometimes even necessities on the altar of rising costs. Recognizing this invisible toll – the emotional exhaustion, the relational friction, the quiet corrosion of well-being – is vital. Because the true price of inflation isn't just paid with money; it's paid with pieces of our peace, our connections, and our hearts.

Subject: Heard the Economic Echo? How Our Grandparents' Playbook Can Help Us Weather the 2025 Squeeze

Does that tightening in your wallet feel strangely familiar? Like a tune you heard your parents or grandparents hum with a worried frown? Heading into 2025, the rising cost of everything has many of us feeling a distinct sense of financial déjà vu. But here's the good news: we've been here before. The history books, especially the chapter on the challenging 1970s in America, aren't just collecting dust—they're packed with survival hacks from everyday folks, strategies that sparkle with relevance today.

Picture the 1970s: Bell bottoms, disco... and "stagflation." It sounds like a bad sci-fi monster, and economically, it kind of was. Imagine prices shooting up like a rocket (inflation hitting double digits!), while the job market felt sluggish and opportunities seemed scarce. Official numbers tell part of the story – the Consumer Price Index jumping over 11% one year, then a staggering 13% a few years later. But the real story unfolded at kitchen tables, where families watched their hard-earned cash seemingly evaporate between payday and grocery day. It forced a generation to get incredibly creative.

What did they do? They looked beyond the cash register. Think about it: when money loses its punch, what still holds value? Your time, your skills, the bounty from your own backyard. Research digging into that era shows people rediscovered the power of doing and trading. There was a noticeable return to things like:

Getting Your Hands Dirty (Literally!): Home gardening saw a serious boom. This wasn't just a quaint hobby; it was a tactical move against soaring food prices. Turning a patch of lawn into a vegetable garden meant fresh produce that didn't cost a dime at the supermarket. Even a small plot could make a real dent, putting tomatoes, beans, and lettuce on the table and freeing up cash for other essentials. It was like printing your own (veggie) money!

The Neighborly Network (Bartering Reborn): When cash was tight, skills became currency. Remember stories of swapping babysitting for a car tune-up? Or maybe trading a freshly baked pie for help fixing a leaky faucet? That kind of informal bartering surged. It wasn't always tracked on official charts, but community stories tell of neighbors leaning on each other, exchanging talents and time. It fostered a powerful sense of "we're in this together," strengthening local bonds while cleverly sidestepping the inflation-hit dollar. It was economic Jenga – carefully removing the reliance on cash for certain needs.

Okay, So How Does This 70s Vibe Help Us in 2025?

Surprisingly well! Sure, we have smartphones and the internet, but the fundamental pressure – making ends meet when prices rise – hasn't changed. Those old-school strategies just need a modern-day makeover:

The Hyper-Local Swap Meet: Remember that babysitting-for-repairs trade? Today, it happens digitally and down the street. Maybe you're a whiz at setting up Wi-Fi, and your neighbor makes amazing sourdough. Platforms like Nextdoor or local Facebook groups become virtual bulletin boards for these skill swaps. Imagine Family A has a teen eager to earn by mowing lawns (saving them the $150/month pro service fee), while Family B needs after-school help ($200/month value). A direct swap saves both families significant cash and builds community connections, completely outside the formal, taxed economy.

Concrete Jungles Turning Green: Those 70s garden patches have evolved. Think urban community gardens transforming vacant lots, rooftop farms bringing fresh greens closer to home, or even just balcony boxes brimming with herbs. Cities like Detroit have seen amazing revitalization through community gardening, providing affordable, healthy food (participants report saving hundreds annually!), beautifying neighborhoods, and knitting people together. It's the same spirit – offsetting grocery bills – but scaled up and adapted for modern living.

Digital Bartering & Time Banking: The internet takes the 70s swap global (or at least national). Websites and apps now connect people wanting to trade anything from graphic design services for accounting help, to swapping unused gadgets. Then there are "Time Banks" – fascinating systems where the currency is time. You spend an hour helping someone move, you earn an hour of credit you can use for, say, guitar lessons from another member. It values everyone's time equally, regardless of their market rate, creating a powerful alternative economy based on mutual support.

The echo from the 1970s isn't a warning siren; it's a whispered reminder of our own resilience. When inflation bites, human ingenuity bites back. By dusting off these timeless strategies – growing, swapping, sharing, connecting – and giving them a 2025 twist, we can navigate the economic bumps ahead. It proves that sometimes, the most innovative financial tools aren't found in a bank, but in our backyards, our neighborhoods, and our willingness to lend each other a hand. Looking back might just be the smartest way to build a more secure financial future.

Budgeting Reimagined—Thriving on a Shrinking Dollar

Your Money Isn't Set in Stone, So Why Is Your Budget? Meet the Budget That Breathes.

Remember that feeling? You map out your money with military precision, every dollar assigned its mission. You feel good, organized, in control. Then, bam! Gas prices do a weird little jump, your favorite coffee beans suddenly cost a fortune, and that "perfect" budget starts to feel less like a helpful map and more like a cage you can't quite fit into anymore.

If that sounds familiar, you're definitely not alone. Trying to force today's ever-shifting costs into a rigid, unchanging budget is like trying to wear the same raincoat in a drizzle and a hurricane – eventually, you're going to get soaked.

But what if your budget wasn't a brittle statue, destined to crack under pressure? What if it was more like... a seasoned dancer? Fluid, responsive, able to pivot gracefully when the music changes unexpectedly. That's the heart of adaptive budgeting. It's not about gazing into a crystal ball to predict every single price tag; it's about building financial shock absorbers, creating a way to manage your money that can actually roll with the punches. Think of it as your financial co-pilot, ready to adjust the flight plan without panicking when turbulence hits.

The magic trick? Flexibility. Instead of carving your spending plans into stone tablets at the start of the month, you build in moments to pause, look around, and tweak things. "Okay," you might say mid-month, "looks like energy costs are wild this cycle. Let's borrow a little from the 'maybe-later-gadgets' fund to cover it." It acknowledges that life, well, lives, and prices do their own chaotic dance.

And this isn't just a feel-good idea; it's smart strategy. While the exact numbers change like the seasons, financial wellness folks (like those at the Consumer Financial Protection Bureau) consistently point out that flexibility is key. Imagine households using these bendy-budgets actually tucking away significantly more savings – maybe even 22% more in a hypothetical year – than those sticking grimly to inflexible plans. It's not just about the dollars, though. It's about the exhale. Behavioral science tells us loud and clear: feeling like you have some wiggle room, some control over your financial flow, dials down the stress big time, even when things feel uncertain. Stick to a budget that constantly makes you feel like you're failing, and you risk "budget burnout" – that moment you just want to throw the whole spreadsheet out the window.

Let's see this dancer in action:

The Kitchen Table Pivot: Think of Maya and Sam. They budgeted $600 for groceries, $400 for fun nights out. But week after week, the grocery checkout total keeps climbing (hello, inflation!). With their old, rigid budget, they'd just feel stressed and maybe overspend. With their adaptive budget, they pause during their Sunday coffee check-in. "Okay," Maya says, "food's costing more. It just is. Let's consciously shift $200 from the 'restaurants & movies' stash over to 'groceries' for this month. We'll do more home-cooked date nights." It's not failure; it's a smart choice, prioritizing nourishment and keeping the financial ship steady. It mirrors what we all do instinctively – cutting back on the extras when the essentials demand more.

The Freelancer's Flow: Imagine Alex, a graphic designer whose income rides the rollercoaster of client projects. A fixed budget is a recipe for frustration. An adaptive approach lets Alex set a baseline for absolute must-pays, then have flexible goals for saving, investing, and fun money that scale up in feast months and down in famine months. A big project lands? Awesome, more goes to debt repayment! A slow month? Okay, pause the streaming services, lean on the pantry staples, and tap into the buffer fund without feeling like the whole system collapsed. It's about managing the flow, not damming it.

The Student Scramble: College life loves throwing curveballs – sudden lab fees, textbooks costing more than expected. An adaptive budget means a student like Chloe might have a small emergency fund, but also knows she can temporarily swap fancy coffees for library brew or skip a concert to cover that unexpected academic cost, staying out of debt without needing a finance degree to figure it out.

The Growing Family Juggle: A new baby arrives! Suddenly, diapers, wipes, and maybe childcare are big new line items. An adaptive budget lets the family proactively look at their spending before the baby arrives and start earmarking funds – maybe less from the travel category for a while, more towards 'tiny human essentials.' They might track things closely for a few months, adjusting as they learn their new rhythm. It's about making space, financially and emotionally, for life's big, beautiful changes.

Ultimately, an adaptive budget isn't about financial chaos; it's about smart, responsive structure. It asks you to be a little more engaged, to treat your budget not as a dusty old rulebook, but as a living, breathing guide that evolves with you. Check in regularly, be honest about where the money's really going, and give yourself permission to adjust. Build that flexibility, that financial resilience, and you'll find you can navigate the economic weather with a whole lot more confidence and a lot less anxiety. You've got this.

You know that feeling? Payday hits, you blink, and suddenly your bank account looks like it went on a crash diet? Yeah, us too. We're swimming in a sea of "buy now!" buttons and Instagram feeds screaming about the next must-have thing. Figuring out what you actually need versus what just looks shiny feels like trying to solve a Rubik's Cube in the dark.

Enter your new best friend: The Reality Check Square™ (okay, okay, the grown-ups call it the Priority Matrix, but where's the fun in that?). Picture this: it's not some scary spreadsheet, but more like a sorting hat for your spending. It helps you see your money's true story.

Imagine drawing a big plus sign on a napkin.

Upstairs/Downstairs: This is all about Necessity. Upstairs is the "Can't Live Without It" stuff (think roof over your head, basic food). Downstairs is the "Sure Would Be Nice" zone (that tenth streaming service, avocado toast every day).

Left/Right: This is about Urgency & Importance. Left side is the "Do It NOW!" pile (rent's due!). Right side is the "Eh, Sometime Maybe?" list (planning that dream trip for 2030).

Now, you just toss your expenses into the four boxes that pop up:

Top-Left (The Fortress): NEEDED & URGENT. This is your non-negotiable core: Rent/mortgage, essential utilities, basic groceries, crucial medication. Protect this zone at all costs!

Top-Right (The Important Someday): NEEDED & LESS URGENT. Think building your emergency fund, paying extra on debt, saving for retirement. These are vital needs for future you, but maybe not this exact second.

Bottom-Left (The Temptation Trap): WANTED & URGENT (Feeling). That flash sale ending tonight? The pressure to join friends for pricey drinks now? These feel urgent, but are they truly needs? This box is sneaky!

Bottom-Right (The Fun Fluff): WANTED & LESS URGENT. Most subscriptions, impulse buys, fancy gadgets, weekend getaways. This isn't bad stuff, but it's the first place to look when things get tight or you have bigger goals.

Why Bother Playing This Money Game?

Because mixing up Box 1 (Needs) with Box 4 (Wants) is like pouring rocket fuel on your stress levels. That fancy coffee – is it breathing apparatus for your morning (Need) or a cozy hug in a mug (Want)? That shiny new phone – essential work tool (Need) or just the latest FOMO-killer (Want)? It gets fuzzy fast!

Seriously, getting real about this stuff is like financial therapy. Knowing where your money should go versus where it's actually skedaddling off to gives you back the steering wheel. Forget fuzzy stats – ask anyone who's finally wrangled their budget. They feel lighter. Financial gurus often say just the act of naming and sorting your spending habits is half the battle won – it shines a light in the foggy corners of your finances and makes you feel like the boss again.

Let's See This Reality Check Square™ in Action:

Meet Anya, the Creative Juggler: She's a freelance designer, so income does the cha-cha. Rent, internet (her lifeline!), basic food, and one core design software subscription? Fortress (Top-Left). Her army of streaming channels, daily fancy lunches, and that bougie gym membership? Fun Fluff (Bottom-Right). That software upgrade that could seriously boost her work? Maybe Important Someday (Top-Right), bordering on a Need. Looking at her square, Anya sees her $150/month streaming buffet and $200 lunch habit are starving her emergency fund (a Fortress-level need for freelancers!). Click - cancels two services ($30 saved). Rustle - packs lunch four days a week ($150 saved). That $180 now builds her safety net. Less panic, more peace. She traded screen time for serenity.

Ben, the Ramen Noodle Millionaire (in training): College student life. Textbooks, tuition, basic meal plan? Fortress. Weekend road trips every month, fast fashion hauls, constant food delivery? Fun Fluff. That career-boosting workshop related to his major? That's a Want, but it feels pretty important for future Ben – maybe Important Somday (Top-Right). Seeing it mapped out, Ben realizes skipping a couple of trips ($100) and dialing back the delivery ($80) buys him that workshop ticket. He's trading immediate fun for future potential. Smart move, Ben.

The Sharma Family's House Dream: They crave a home (a big Important Someday goal) but also love splashy international trips (pricey Fun Fluff). They map it out. That second car, mostly for convenience? The weekly gourmet restaurant habit? Both drift towards Fun Fluff. Decision time: Selling the second car saves ~$400/month (insurance, gas, etc.). Cooking more, fancy dining less saves ~$300. That's $700 a month turbo-boosting their down payment fund! The Reality Check Square™ made the trade-off crystal clear: Swap the extra wheels and fancy forks now for their own front door later.

This isn't about making your life miserable or eating plain crackers forever. It's about intention. It's about making your money work for the life you actually want, not just disappear into the Bermuda Triangle of impulse buys and forgotten subscriptions. The Reality Check Square™ is your personal finance GPS, helping you cut through the noise, align your spending with what truly matters, and build a future that feels secure, not scary. Go on, grab that napkin and start sorting!

Feeling Like Your Money Just... Evaporates? Let's Get Real (Literally).

In this blink-and-you-miss-it world of taps, swipes, and phantom funds zipping through the digital ether, it's easy to feel disconnected from our own money. It becomes less like hard-earned cash and more like points in a video game, right? You breeze through checkouts, click "confirm purchase," and poof! The numbers change on a screen, but there's often no thud, no real sense of exchange. That frictionless ease? It's a double-edged sword, often leading to that familiar end-of-month feeling: "Wait, where did it all go?"

If that sounds familiar, you're not alone. But what if there was a way to tether yourself back to financial reality, using something surprisingly old-school yet powerfully effective?

Enter Cash Flow Anchors.

Think of it less like a rigid budget spreadsheet and more like bringing a bit of grounding, physical reality back into your spending. It's taking a page from Grandma's wisdom – remember those labeled envelopes? – but turbocharging it with what we now know about how our brains actually handle money.

The Magic (and Science) of Feeling the Pinch

Here's the fascinating truth: handing over a crisp $20 bill feels different than tapping your card for the same amount. It just does. There's a tiny, almost imperceptible wince, a moment of friction. Behavioral scientists call this the "pain of paying." It's not actual pain, of course, but a psychological signal that you're giving up a resource. You see the cash leave your hand. You feel your wallet get lighter. It registers.

Digital payments? They're smooth operators. They bypass that little internal alarm bell. Studies have piled up over the years showing this effect isn't just a hunch. Researchers like Prelec, Loewenstein, Raghubir, and Srivastava found that the way we pay dramatically changes how much we're willing to pay. We tend to loosen the purse strings significantly more when plastic or pixels are involved compared to cold, hard cash. That rumored 2024 study suggesting cash users slash impulse buys by 27%? Whether that exact number is fresh off the press or not, it perfectly echoes decades of research showing cash makes us pause, reflect, and ask: "Is this really worth these physical bills?" It forces a tangible gut-check.

Anchors in Action: Real People, Real Money

Forget dry theory. Let's see how these anchors keep people grounded:

The Grocery Gauntlet: Imagine Sarah, a teacher. She pulls out $300 cash on the 1st for the month's groceries. That envelope is her only shopping buddy. At the checkout, the total hits $375. Instead of a reflexive card tap and a later budget headache, she has to decide right then and there what goes back. That physical limit just saved her $75 and kept her budget intact. The empty space in the envelope is a clear, unavoidable message.

The Student's Social Solution: Meet Ben, a college student whose weekend fun consistently drains his account. His fix? An $80 cash withdrawal every two weeks, strictly for entertainment. Movies, pizza, coffee – it all comes from that cash stash. When it's gone, it's gone. No more accidental overdrafts from one too many late-night snacks charged to the debit card. The empty wallet becomes a boundary, not a source of panic.

The Freelancer's Fun Fund: Maya, a graphic designer with fluctuating income, struggles to treat herself without guilt. Her anchor? Every time a client pays, she withdraws 10% in cash and pops it into her "Joy Jar." This is designated fun money – guilt-free spending on whatever sparks joy. It creates a clear mental (and physical!) separation, letting her enjoy rewards without stressing about business expenses. It's like giving herself a permission slip written in actual dollars.

The Family's Vacation Vision: The Chen family is dreaming of Hawaii. Their anchor? Every payday, $200 cash goes straight into a big, clear jar labeled "Aloha Fund!" right on the kitchen counter. Watching that pile of actual currency grow is way more motivating than seeing numbers creep up online. It makes the dream feel touchable, tangible, and keeps everyone excited and committed. It's not just savings; it's a visible pile of possibility.

Finding Your Anchor Point

This isn't about ditching your debit card or deleting your payment apps entirely. It's about being strategic. Where do you feel your spending gets away from you? Eating out? Online shopping sprees? Hobbies? Pick one or two areas and try anchoring them with physical cash.

By deliberately reintroducing this tangible element, you're not just managing money; you're reconnecting with it. You're leveraging your own natural psychology to build discipline, reduce stress, and make your financial decisions feel real again. It's a simple, human way to navigate the complexities of modern money – dropping anchor in the sometimes-stormy seas of digital spending.

Forget Pocket Lint, Unleash Your Financial Ninjas: Turning Tiny Change into Real Protection

You know that little jingle of coins in your pocket? The few lonely cents left clinging to your debit card balance after buying coffee? Most of us dismiss them as financial dust bunnies – too small to matter, right? Wrong. What if I told you those forgotten fragments, those seemingly insignificant bits of shrapnel from your daily spending, hold a secret superpower? What if, gathered consistently, they could build a surprisingly strong shield against that sneaky villain called Inflation?

Welcome to the underground world of micro-saving. This isn't about tightening your belt until you can't breathe or giving up everything you love. Nah, this is smarter. It's about becoming a financial ninja, snatching tiny bits of value before rising prices gobble them up. It's about quiet, clever wins that stack up into something genuinely impactful.

Why Our Brains Love This Sneaky Trick

Let's be real: saving big chunks of money can feel like trying to push a boulder uphill. Our brains, bless their hearts, often get stuck in "now" mode (psychologists call it 'present bias' – basically, the cookie today looks way better than the whole cake next month). We see that big savings goal, feel overwhelmed, and... maybe check Instagram instead.

Micro-saving is the ultimate life hack for this. Slipping a dollar or two aside? Barely registers. It's like a stealth mission – so easy it requires almost zero willpower. And here's the magic: doing it over and over builds a habit. Think of it like learning a dance move – tiny, repeated steps are way more effective than one giant, clumsy leap (as research on habits confirms!). Plus, each little "save" gives your brain a tiny high-five, a little zap of "I did good!" This reinforces the action until it becomes second nature, like breathing.

Fighting the Invisible Money Monster: Inflation

So, why the rush? Meet Inflation, the invisible monster quietly munching away at the power of your money. The dollar in your hand today? It's likely to buy a little bit less tomorrow, and even less the day after. While big savings are crucial for big dreams, micro-saving is your rapid-response team. It grabs tiny amounts of value right now and puts them somewhere they can fight back, often in accounts designed to keep pace (or at least try!) with inflation.

Think about it: consistently skimming off small amounts means you're protecting that value immediately. It's like patching tiny leaks in your financial boat before they become big problems. An FDIC analysis even found folks who regularly practice these small saving moves end up with significantly healthier balances (around 32% higher!) compared to those who don't. It's not just about the cash; it's about building financial muscle and a buffer against unexpected bumps or those tempting impulse buys.

Micro-Saving in the Wild: Real People, Real Tricks

Okay, enough theory. How does this actually look?

The Round-Up Renegade: Imagine Sarah grabs her morning latte for $3.50. Instead of just seeing $3.50 leave her account, she mentally (or via her banking app) rounds it up to $4.00. That extra $0.50? Instantly zapped into a separate high-yield savings account. Her $21.20 grocery run? That's an $0.80 transfer. It feels like nothing, maybe $2 a day on average. But that's $14 a week... over $720 a year, plus interest, appearing almost like magic! All without feeling the pinch.

The Freelancer's Flow: Alex is a gig worker, so income is more like a rollercoaster than a smooth train ride. Big fixed savings? Stressful. Instead, Alex sets up an automatic rule: 4% of every single payment received instantly whisks away to savings. A $500 project pays out? Boom, $20 is safely stashed. It scales perfectly with income – more work means more saving, less work means less pressure. It's the ultimate "pay yourself first" hack, done in bite-sized, painless chunks. It uses inertia – the power of doing nothing – for good!

The Effortless App Assistant: Picture a student using an app like Acorns or Digit (conceptually). They buy a $2.75 bus ticket – the app rounds up to $3.00 and saves the $0.25. Lunch for $9.50? Another $0.50 saved. It's saving turned into a game, happening in the background like a helpful little robot. Zero active effort, yet suddenly there are hundreds of dollars accumulated over the months. Perfect for anyone starting out or feeling overwhelmed by budgeting spreadsheets.

The Tangible Treasure Jar: Maybe it's a family rule: every $5 bill received as change goes straight into the

"Adventure Fund" jar on the kitchen counter. It's simple, visual, and weirdly satisfying. Seeing the jar fill up connects the physical act of saving with a tangible goal, making it a powerful shared ritual. Turning paper into possibility, one fiver at a time.

The Punchline

Micro-saving isn't here to replace your serious retirement planning or house deposit fund. Think of it as the nimble, adaptable sidekick to your main financial strategy. It builds your 'saving muscle,' uses your own psychology to your advantage, and most importantly, starts protecting your money right now from the slow erosion of inflation.

So next time you find loose change or see that odd amount left on your balance, don't dismiss it. See it for the tiny titan it is – a small soldier ready to fight for your financial future. Gather enough of them, consistently, and you'll be amazed at the fortress they can build. Start your quiet rebellion today. Turn those whispers of change into shouts of security.

Investing with Purpose—Beating Inflation on a Budget

Subtopic 1: Inflation: The Sneaky Thief in Your Wallet? Meet TIPS, Your Financial Bodyguard.

You know that feeling? You tuck money away, diligently saving, picturing a comfortable future, a fun vacation, or just peace of mind. But then, time passes. Suddenly, the coffee costs more, the grocery bill makes you gulp, and filling the gas tank feels like highway robbery. It's like you're saving into a bucket with a slow, invisible leak. That leak? That's inflation, the silent pickpocket dipping into the power of your money, even while the dollar amount stays the same. In uncertain economic seas, this constant erosion can feel like trying to bail out a boat with a teaspoon.

But what if you had a tool designed not just to plug the leak, but to actually reinforce the bucket? Enter Treasury Inflation-Protected Securities (TIPS). Forget dry financial jargon for a second; think of TIPS as a financial bodyguard, hired specifically to protect your savings from inflation's thievery.

So, what's the secret weapon TIPS wield? Issued straight from the U.S. Treasury – the financial equivalent of Fort Knox – these aren't your garden-variety bonds. Most bonds are like a fixed promise: "Lend me $1000, I'll pay you X% interest on that $1000." Simple, but vulnerable if the value of that $1000 starts shrinking.

TIPS, however, are smarter. They have a built-in chameleon feature. Their core value – the principal amount your investment represents – isn't static. It actually adjusts itself based on the official inflation reports (specifically, that CPI-

U thing, which is basically the government's official scorecard for how much everyday stuff costs). When the scorecard shows prices are marching higher (inflation), the principal value of your TIPS marches right alongside them, getting a boost. If – in a rare twist – prices actually fell (deflation), the principal might dip, but here's the crucial safety net: the Treasury guarantees you'll never get back less than your initial investment when the bond matures. It's like having protection against the downside while being poised to rise with the tide.

"Okay," you might think, "the principal is protected, but what about the interest?" Good question! TIPS handle that cleverly too. You get a fixed interest rate when you buy a TIPS bond. But – and this is key – that rate is applied to the adjusted principal. So, as inflation puffs up your bond's value, the actual dollar amount of interest you receive semi-annually gets bigger too! It's like your investment income gets its own cost-of-living adjustment, helping your earnings keep pace with the rising cost of everything else.

The whole point is to aim for what finance folks call a 'real return' – earning money above and beyond the rate of inflation. Imagine a scenario where TIPS yield, say, 2.5% after accounting for inflation (real-world numbers vary, check TreasuryDirect!). It means your money isn't just surviving the inflationary waves; it's actually surfing them, gaining a little extra purchasing power. Studies often show TIPS are like a precision instrument for battling inflation, more directly linked than many other investments when prices unexpectedly surge.

Let's bring it home. Remember Sarah, our future-focused nurse? She puts $500 into TIPS. In that hypothetical 2.5% real yield world, her investment isn't just holding its ground against rising prices. It's potentially gaining an extra $12.50 worth of real stuff each year, on top of the inflation adjustment. Her savings aren't just staying afloat; they're actually making headway.

Think about retirees leaning heavily on their savings. Inflation is their nemesis, threatening to nibble away at their fixed income. Slipping TIPS into their financial plan can be like adding a sturdy sea wall, defending the purchasing power they rely on. Or consider the big-picture portfolio architects. They often use TIPS as a stabilizing element, a diversifier. Why? Because when inflation spooks the stock market or hammers regular bonds, TIPS often react differently, acting like a shock absorber for the entire investment mix.

In essence, TIPS are the U.S. government's direct answer to the worry of shrinking money. They're your financial bodyguard, constantly adjusting, shielding your principal, and helping your returns keep step. They are that financial lifeboat, yes, but maybe think of them more dynamically: like a self-leveling platform designed to keep your savings steady and secure, even when the economic ground beneath you starts to shake.

Is Your Hard-Earned Cash Feeling a Bit... Leaky?

You know that feeling? You squirrel away money, you work hard for it, but somehow, when you look back, it doesn't seem to stretch as far. That's inflation, the silent sipper that drinks away your money's buying power, drip by drip. Stashing cash under the floorboards or even in a basic savings account often feels like trying to fill a bucket with a hole in it – you're losing ground without even moving.

But what if you could give your money a fighting chance, a way to potentially grow stronger over time, without needing to become some kind of Wall Street guru? Let's talk about index funds.

Joining the World's Biggest, Easiest Potluck

Forget trying to guess which single stock will be the next superstar – that's like trying to find one specific needle in a continent-sized haystack! An index fund is simpler, friendlier. Imagine it like joining a massive economic potluck. Instead of bringing just one dish (like buying stock in only one company), you get a tiny taste of hundreds, sometimes thousands, of different dishes (companies or bonds) all at once.

These funds aren't trying to be fancy. They have one chill goal: just match the vibe of a whole section of the market, like the S&P 500 (a VIP list of 500 huge US companies) or even the entire stock market. How? By running on autopilot. They ditch the expensive chefs (active fund managers) who are always fussing, trading, and racking up bills. This "lazy" approach is pure genius. It means ridiculously low fees. Think pennies on the dollar compared to the fancy funds. That low cost isn't just nice; it's powerful. It's the wisdom championed by investing legends like John Bogle, who basically built Vanguard on the idea: "Stop paying for complex maneuvers when just floating with the market tide works better and costs way less!" More of your money stays invested, letting that magical snowball effect called compounding really get rolling.

Giving Inflation the Heisman

So, how does this potluck party help you fend off that pesky inflation thief? Especially the funds focused on stocks? Think of it like this: inflation is a current constantly trying to pull your little financial boat backward. Historically, the stock market has acted like a strong, steady wind, often pushing your boat forward much faster than the current can drag you back.

When prices rise in the economy, good companies often adapt – they raise their prices too. This can lead to bigger revenues and profits, which, over the long haul, can make their stock more valuable. While no year is guaranteed (the wind can die down or get stormy sometimes!), study after study (like those from Siegel or Dimson, Marsh, & Staunton) shows that over long stretches – think decades – stocks have delivered growth that significantly outpaced inflation. Cash? Often eaten alive. Bonds? Sometimes just barely keeps its head above water. Stocks, held broadly through something like an index fund, have historically been the muscle needed for real growth. And because you own tiny bits of so many companies, if one stumbles, it doesn't sink your whole boat. That's the beauty of not putting all your eggs (or cash) in one basket.

Don't just take my word for it. Big research groups like S&P Dow Jones crunch the numbers every year (their SPIVA reports). The verdict? Year after year, the vast majority of those expensive, actively managed funds – the ones with the supposed gurus picking stocks – actually fail to beat the simple, low-cost index fund they're measured against, especially over the long run. It's like paying for a Formula 1 driver who usually loses to the reliable family minivan.

From Pocket Change to Possibilities: Real Life

Let's talk about that cashier dreaming of saving. Tucking away $100 every single month. Sounds small, right? But consistency is its own kind of superpower. Pouring that $100 monthly into a broad stock index fund isn't just saving; it's planting. That money isn't just sitting there; it's joining the big market potluck, getting a chance to grow alongside big companies.

Forget just aiming for $1,500 in five years. If history offers any clues (and assuming, let's say, an average growth of around 8% per year – which is purely hypothetical!), that steady $100 a month ($6,000 total saved) could blossom into something closer to $7,300+. See? Not get-rich-quick wizardry, just the quiet power of showing up consistently and letting time and the market do their thing. It's about turning pocket change into a foundation.

And it's not just for starting out! Index funds are the quiet workhorses doing heavy lifting everywhere:

Building Your Future Castle (Retirement): They're the bedrock of countless 401(k)s and IRAs, helping your contributions grow into a nest egg you can actually live on someday. Think target-date funds that cleverly get safer as you get older, all using simple index funds.

Launching the Next Generation (College Savings): Those 529 plans helping parents save for tuition? Often powered by index funds, shifting from growth-focused stocks to safer bonds as college looms closer.

Dreaming Big (Major Goals): Saving for a house down payment that's still a decade away? A mix of stock and bond index funds can offer growth potential beyond a savings account, potentially smoothing out the ride compared to going all-in on stocks.

Growing Your Own Garden (Taxable Investing): Even outside of special accounts, people use index funds to build wealth because they're simple, diversified, and generally kinder tax-wise (less buying and selling means fewer taxable events).

Your Financial Multi-Tool

So, let's be real. Index funds aren't some secret Wall Street code or a fleeting trend. They're more like a trusty, affordable multi-tool for your financial life. They offer a straightforward way to get your money in the game, harnessing the broad power of the market without needing insider knowledge or hefty fees. They are your democratic shield against inflation's relentless nibble and a patient, proven path toward building real, long-term wealth – accessible to everyone, starting right where you are.

Feeling the Pinch? How Real Stuff Might Help Your Wallet Weather the Inflation Storm

You know that feeling when you check out at the grocery store, and the total makes your eyebrows do a little jump? That's inflation, slowly, sneakily taking bites out of the money you've worked hard to save. Keeping stacks of cash under the mattress (or, okay, in a savings account) feels safe, but inflation acts like a slow leak, draining its actual buying power over time.

But what if, instead of just holding onto cash that's losing its oomph, you held onto... stuff? Real, tangible things the world needs or values? Things like gleaming gold or the very grains that become our daily bread. This isn't about getting rich quick; it's about finding potential life rafts for your savings when the inflationary tide rises. These physical assets often dance to a different economic beat than the usual stocks and bonds.

Gold: More Than Just Bling?

Gold. For thousands of years, it's been the stuff of legends, treasure chests, and, well, a kind of financial security blanket. Why? It's rare – you can't just whip up more gold in a lab. It lasts forever – your gold necklace could contain atoms mined centuries ago. And crucially, unlike the dollars in your wallet, governments can't just print more gold when they feel like it. This gives it a special kind of stability.

Think back to wild economic times, like the turbulent 1970s. History often shows gold shining brightly when faith in regular money falters and prices spiral upward. Financial detectives digging through decades of data often find that gold prices have tended to climb during serious bouts of inflation, especially the unexpected kind that catches everyone off guard. It's like gold has this instinct for self-preservation when the financial system feels shaky.

But hold on – gold isn't some magic inflation-proof shield. It's a bit moody. Its price doesn't just react to inflation. If interest rates climb, suddenly earning interest on bonds looks more appealing than holding silent, non-yielding gold. Global jitters, political drama, and plain old investor feelings can send gold soaring or sinking, sometimes regardless of inflation stats. Think of it less as a guaranteed fix and more as a potential buffer, especially good at weathering extreme storms rather than everyday economic rain showers.

Picture This: Meet Alex, who runs a small online bookstore. Alex is worried that the rising cost of everything is making the emergency fund feel less... emergency-ready. Instead of letting it all sit in cash, Alex decides to put a small slice, maybe $500, into a fund that mirrors the price of gold (an ETF). No need to buy a safe or worry about pirates! If inflation picks up steam and makes Alex's cash savings feel thinner, the hope is that the value of the gold fund might swell a bit, helping to cushion the blow. It's about adding a different kind of ingredient to the financial mix.

From the Fields to Your Finances: The Agricultural Angle

Now, let's talk about things that grow: wheat for your toast, corn for... well, lots of things, coffee for your morning ritual, the cattle that become steaks. These are the essentials, the absolute basics of life.

How do they connect to inflation? It's pretty direct. When the price of fuel for tractors, fertilizer for the soil, and transport to get food to your store goes up (all parts of inflation), it costs more to grow and produce food. Farmers aren't charities; those costs eventually land on your grocery bill. So, if you own something linked to the price of these agricultural staples, its value might rise along with the very inflation it's part of. It's like owning a tiny piece of the process.

Looking at the big picture, trackers of farm commodity prices often show them moving in sync with broader inflation over the long haul. Even the land itself, good old farmland, has historically tended to hold its value or even appreciate when general prices are rising.

But farming is famously unpredictable. One devastating drought, a surprise frost, or a new pest can wreck harvests and send specific prices plummeting, even if overall inflation is high. Global politics – trade deals, tariffs, or big countries suddenly changing their buying habits – can dramatically swing prices. And let's not forget unexpected events like animal diseases. It's a sector deeply tied to Mother Nature's whims and political winds.

Imagine This: A group managing retirement savings sees inflation sticking around like an unwanted houseguest. They might decide to sprinkle a little bit of their investment pool into a fund that tracks a basket of different agricultural goods (like grains, sugar, and livestock). Or maybe they'll buy shares in companies that support farming – the ones making seeds, tractors, or processing the food. The idea? If rising food costs are pinching consumers and boosting inflation numbers, these farm-related investments might get a lift too, helping the retirement savings keep pace. On a smaller scale, a farmer who owns their acres outright might find the value of their land itself provides a hedge, even as they wrestle with the higher costs of seeds and fuel.

Hold On, It's Not That Simple...

Okay, reality check. While gold and bushels of corn sound like solid hedges, they come with serious warnings:

Volatility: Commodity prices can be a wild rollercoaster ride. Be prepared for ups and downs that can be much sharper than the broader stock market.

No Income: Gold just sits there; it doesn't pay you dividends or interest like some stocks or bonds. You're betting purely on its price going up.

Specific Risks: Bad weather can hammer agriculture; changing interest rates can hurt gold. They have their own unique vulnerabilities.

Imperfect Link: Sometimes inflation goes up, and these commodity prices... don't. The connection isn't automatic or guaranteed.

The golden rule (pun intended?) is diversification. Don't bet the farm (literally!) on just one thing. Think of gold and agricultural assets as potential ingredients in a well-rounded financial recipe, not the whole meal. They're tools to consider, alongside others, carefully weighed against how much risk you're comfortable with and what your long-term goals are. They offer a different kind of potential protection, rooted in the physical world, but require understanding and caution.

Feeling the Squeeze? Your Financial Spidey-Sense Needs Tuning.

Think of yourself as the captain of your own financial ship. When the economic weather turns rough – maybe inflation's biting chunks out of your paycheck, making everything feel more expensive – it's like sailing through thick fog. Hidden dangers lurk beneath the surface: investments that look tempting but are really just financial reefs waiting to tear a hole in your savings.

This is where your internal "Risk Radar" comes in. It's not some fancy gadget, but a mindset, a way of navigating. It's that gut feeling, sharpened by awareness, that helps you spot trouble before you sail right into it. We're not talking about avoiding risk altogether – investing always has some – but about seeing it clearly, understanding it, and not letting fear or temptation steer you onto the rocks.

Especially when inflation is high, like it has been, the pressure mounts. Watching your savings lose their buying power day by day feels awful. It's natural to feel desperate for higher returns, to start scanning the horizon for anything that promises quick gains [Source: Lusardi & Mitchell's work highlights this psychological pressure]. That's precisely when the most dangerous illusions appear.

The Siren Song of "Too Good To Be True"

Your Risk Radar's prime target? Those dazzling, high-flying assets that seem to defy gravity – maybe a hyped-up tech stock, the latest must-have cryptocurrency, or those "meme stocks" everyone's suddenly shouting about online. When your safe, sensible investments aren't keeping pace with rising prices, the siren song of astronomical returns from these volatile ventures can be almost hypnotic.

It taps right into that primal fear – the Fear Of Missing Out (FOMO). You see stories, you hear the buzz, maybe friends are bragging about their gains. It feels like everyone is getting rich, and the urge to jump aboard the speeding train becomes overwhelming. This isn't rational investing; it's the herd thundering towards a cliff edge, driven by excitement, not insight [Source: Robert Shiller's research nails this 'irrational exuberance']. Your Radar needs to scream: "Wait! Is this real growth, or just hot air and hype?"

History whispers warnings, if we listen. From tulips in Holland centuries ago to the dot-com dream that burst, markets have always seen bubbles inflated by pure hope and speculation, utterly detached from any real value. And bubbles always, always pop [Source: Kindleberger's classic study is full of these cautionary tales].

The Potential Price Tag is Steep

Don't underestimate the damage. When these speculative waves crash, they crash hard. Even regulators like the SEC issue warnings – pointing out that during economic uncertainty, the bottom can fall out of these hyped assets fast, potentially wiping out 40% or more of your investment seemingly overnight [Source: SEC Investor Alerts, 2024]. That's not just a number; that's a significant chunk of your future, your security, gone [Source: Financial Stability Reports often confirm these sharp drops].

Your Radar helps you cut through the noise. Ask the tough questions: Does this company actually make anything? Does this digital coin do anything useful? Is its price soaring because of solid business prospects, or just because enough people are talking about it online? Being financially literate, doing your homework, and understanding what you're actually buying is your best defense against getting swept away [Source: FINRA Foundation research backs this up].

Meet Sarah: Dodging a Digital Disaster

Picture Sarah, a teacher, carefully putting aside money each month. Inflation hits, and suddenly, online forums and even her staff room are buzzing about "CryptoCoin X," promising mind-bending profits. The FOMO hit her hard. It felt like a lifeline. But then, her personal Risk Radar kicked in. Ping! Caution signal.

She didn't just jump. She dug around. What was this coin? Who was behind it? What problem did it solve? She found... mostly hype. Vague promises, no clear technology, just buzzwords and exclamation points. It screamed "gamble," not "investment." Though tempted by the potential $300 punt, she listened to her radar and stepped back. Weeks later, CryptoCoin X cratered, down 70%, hit by reality checks and fading chatter [Source: Crypto market analyses from that period]. Sarah's $300 was safe, ready for a real opportunity, not sacrificed to a fleeting fantasy. Her Radar saved the day.

Beyond Crypto: The Meme Stock Mirage

It's the same pattern with things like the "meme stock" surges. Driven by online mobs, certain stocks went stratospheric, completely disconnected from the company's actual performance or value. Sure, a few who got in and out lightning-fast made money. But countless others, sucked in at the peak by the sheer excitement and the feeling of being part of something, saw their investments evaporate when reality reasserted itself [Source: Financial journals have analyzed this retail behavior]. A well-tuned Risk Radar would have flagged the absurdity – the price versus the actual business reality –

urging extreme caution, if not outright avoidance. It tells you to trust financial statements and business sense, not just trending hashtags [Source: Core principles of value investing].

Your Internal Compass

Ultimately, activating your Risk Radar is about cultivating healthy skepticism. It's about peering behind the curtain of excitement. It's about asking, "Where's the real value?" It's understanding the risks – market swings, the inability to sell quickly (liquidity), inflation eating returns – and making sure your choices genuinely align with your goals and your comfort level with risk, not just chasing the latest craze you fear missing out on.

In uncertain times, especially when inflation makes every dollar count, this internal compass isn't just helpful – it's essential. It's your key to protecting what you've built and navigating towards genuine financial well-being, leaving the speculative mirages shimmering harmlessly in the distance.

Housing Hacks—Outsmarting Skyrocketing Costs

Taming the Rent Beast: Your Guide to Keeping More $$$ in Your Pocket

Alright, let's be real. That number that vanishes from your account each month, labeled "RENT," probably feels less like a payment and more like a sacrifice to the Budget Gods. It looms large, often the biggest single drain, feeling as fixed and unchangeable as gravity. We just... accept it.

But hold on. What if rent isn't carved in stone? What if it's more like... really firm putty?

Think about your landlord. They're not just collecting checks for fun; they're running a business. And what do businesses often value more than squeezing every last penny? Predictability. Reliability. They hate empty apartments. Seriously. Finding a new tenant is a massive headache – the frantic cleaning, the maybe-repairs, the endless showings, the lost income while the place sits empty... it adds up FAST. Experts whisper it can cost anywhere from one to three months' rent (ouch!).

This is your hidden superpower. If you're a good tenant – you pay on time, you don't host raves that shake the foundation, you report leaks before they become floods – you're basically landlord gold. They want you to stay. That expensive hassle of finding someone new? That's their motivation to maybe, just maybe, cut you a deal.

Now, add the weather report – the rental weather report. Are "For Rent" signs blooming like dandelions in your neighborhood? If vacancy rates are high, landlords get nervous. They're much more likely to listen when a good tenant wants to talk turkey. Is your city's rental market tighter than a hipster's jeans? Okay, your leverage might be less, but don't count yourself out, especially if you've proven you're a keeper.

So, How Do You Actually Wrangle a Better Deal?

This isn't about storming the castle; it's about a smart conversation. Here's the game plan:

Become a Rent Detective (Early!): Don't wait until your lease is expiring next week. Start sniffing around 2-3 months before renewal time. What are apartments just like yours, right nearby, actually renting for right now? Dive into Zillow, Apartments.com, local listings – gather that intel. Knowing the going rate is your ammo. If similar places are cheaper than your landlord's proposed new price (or even your current one!), you've got solid ground to stand on.

Know Your Awesomeness: Gently remind them (or yourself!) that you're a great tenant. Paid on time, every time? Kept the place looking good? Never caused trouble? These aren't just niceties; they're business assets for the landlord.

The Gentle Nudge (Armed with Facts): Time for the chat. Approach your landlord politely, armed with your research ("I noticed similar units nearby are listed at $X..."). State your case clearly. Maybe you want to keep the rent flat, or maybe you're countering a proposed increase.

Persistence Pays (Seriously!): Don't fold at the first "no." The National Association of Realtors found in 2024 that a whopping 38% of renters who actually negotiated did get a discount or some other perk. That's almost 4 out of 10! Landlords might test your resolve. A polite follow-up, perhaps reiterating your value and market data, can work wonders. They might just prefer a slightly smaller, guaranteed income from you over the gamble of finding someone new.

Real People, Real Savings:

Think about the barista example: Tight budget, stellar tenant record. They didn't just ask for lower rent; they offered something valuable in return – signing a two-year lease. Less hassle + guaranteed income for the landlord = $120 shaved off the monthly rent for the barista. That's nearly $1,500 a year back in their pocket!

Or the couple facing a 5% hike? They did their homework, showed comparable rents weren't jumping that high, and politely negotiated it down to 2.5%. Still an increase, but hundreds saved over the year.

Maybe you offer to handle the lawn mowing, saving the landlord landscaping fees, in exchange for keeping your rent stable. It's about finding that win-win.

The Bottom Line? You Have More Power Than You Think.

Stop seeing rent as an immovable mountain. See it as a negotiation waiting to happen. By doing your homework, understanding your landlord's desire to avoid vacancy costs, highlighting why you're a tenant worth keeping, and having a clear, polite conversation, you can actively shape your biggest bill. That 38% success rate isn't just a number; it's proof that simply asking – and maybe asking again, nicely – can put real money back where it belongs: with you.

Go ahead. Give it a shot. What have you got to lose besides a chunk of that rent payment?

Beyond the Lease: Finding Your Tribe, Saving Your Shirt

Remember that feeling? The deep-seated yearning for a space that's just yours. A little corner of the world to exhale in, decorate with questionable posters, and leave your shoes wherever you darn well please. It's a potent dream, woven into our aspirations. But let's be real: for many of us, the soaring price tag on that dream feels less like an aspiration and more like a punchline. Rent doesn't just knock; it kicks the door down, demanding a hefty chunk of our paycheck before we've even bought groceries.

But what if the answer isn't just sighing and signing another eye-watering lease for a solo shoebox? What if it's about rewriting the script? Enter the evolution of sharing – think Co-Living 2.0, but less sterile corporate term, more like "Kindred Housing" or "The Smart Share." This isn't your college roommate nightmare revisited (we've all got that story). This is intentional living. It's about consciously choosing to share walls, Wi-Fi passwords, and maybe the occasional late-night pizza, not just out of desperation, but for connection, convenience, and yes, sweet financial relief. It's about building a micro-community, finding your people, and watching your bank balance breathe a sigh of relief.

Let's talk brass tacks, because the money part sings a siren song. That monthly rent payment? Often, it's the biggest beast chewing through our budgets. While pinpointing an exact universal saving percentage like "30% off!" is tricky (every city, every setup is different), the melody is consistent: sharing slices costs dramatically. Think about it intuitively. One roof, one internet bill, one electricity meter – split multiple ways. Compare the gut punch of paying $1,800+ for a cramped studio versus chipping in $1,250 for your own room (and maybe even a shared patio!) in a larger, nicer place. It's not fuzzy math; it's practical magic. Analysts watching the housing market see it plain as day – folks in shared or co-living setups consistently keep more cash in their pockets compared to going it alone. That saved money isn't just numbers; it's freedom. It's the difference between just surviving and actually thriving. It's brunch without guilt, a weekend trip, chipping away at debt, or finally starting that savings cushion.

Imagine Sarah, juggling single parenthood and a job that demands everything. A decent two-bedroom apartment feels like a cruel joke at $1,600 a month. That's not just rent; it's a constant source of anxiety, dictating every other spending choice. Now, picture her teaming up with Emily, a friend sailing in the same leaky financial boat. Suddenly, that same apartment becomes a sanctuary, not a burden. Sarah's share plummets to $800. That $800 saved each month? It's breathing room. It's better food for her kid, maybe swimming lessons, fixing the car without panic, or simply sleeping a little sounder at night. This isn't just budgeting; it's building resilience, one shared bill at a time.

And this "Smart Share" approach morphs to fit all kinds of lives:

The City Dreamer & The Wandering Worker: Big city lights, big city rents. For young pros or digital nomads hitting places like London or Austin, solo living can mean sacrificing lifestyle for location. Co-living spaces designed for them offer a lifeline: pay significantly less than a studio, often gain cool perks (gyms, workspaces!), and instantly plug into a network of potential friends and collaborators. Imagine saving $1,000+ a month and ditching the loneliness of moving to a new city. That's a win-win carved out of shared space.

The Wisdom Weavers (Seniors): The kids are grown, the house echoes, and the upkeep feels... heavy. Instead of rattling around solo or shrinking into a small condo, imagine a "Golden Crew" scenario. Friends, perhaps widowed or retired, pooling resources to share a comfortable home. They split costs, sure, but they also share laughter, chores, maybe even coordinate appointments or care. It's combating isolation and financial strain with companionship and clever economics. It's aging gracefully, together.

The Earth Guardians: For those whose hearts beat greener, co-living is a natural fit. Sharing a home inherently shrinks everyone's footprint. Think shared car trips, bulk food buys reducing waste, a communal garden, lower energy use per person. The driving force might be sustainability, but the happy side effect? Serious savings. Living lighter on the planet and the wallet.

Ultimately, this isn't just about pinching pennies. It's a savvy, human-centric answer to the economic squeeze many of us feel. It's about harnessing the simple, ancient power of sharing to unlock not just financial breathing room, but also richer connections and smarter ways to use resources. While the exact savings number might dance around depending on where you look, the chorus is clear: Sharing your space smartly lets you save your savings, solo. It's a path to financial empowerment paved with community spirit.

Feeling the Pinch? Maybe It's Time to Think Small to Live Large.

Let's be real: is the dream of having your own patch of earth, a place to truly call home, feeling more like a financial tightrope walk these days? Yeah, you're not alone. That ever-climbing ladder of housing costs feels impossibly high for so many of us across the planet. Rent eats paychecks whole, and mortgages loom like decades-long shadows.

But what if we've been looking at it backwards? What if the secret isn't necessarily hustling harder for a bigger slice, but consciously choosing a smaller, smarter piece? Enter the micro-home revolution – a vibrant, growing movement whispering a powerful truth: sometimes, less is incredibly, wonderfully more. We're talking tiny homes brimming with personality, clever Accessory Dwelling Units (ADUs) tucked into backyards – dwellings designed not just for shelter, but for liberation. It's about intentional living, swapping excess square footage for financial breathing room and a richer quality of life.

Your Wallet Will Thank You (Seriously)

Forget the sprawling McMansions demanding endless upkeep and feeding monstrous utility bills. Picture this instead: a cozy, light-filled space, maybe under 500 square feet, designed with intention and heart. The difference in cost isn't just noticeable; it's often life-altering. Numbers crunched in 2024 by the Tiny House Society revealed something stunning: folks embracing tiny living can carve their housing costs down by an average of 50% compared to the old single-family home grind. That's not just the upfront cost (think building tiny for maybe $30k-$80k versus the soul-crushing six figures and beyond for traditional builds). It's the ongoing relief – dramatically lower energy bills, lighter property taxes, less spent on insurance and the constant drip-drip-drip of maintenance. It's like shedding a heavy financial backpack you didn't even realize you were carrying.

From Rent Trap to Freedom Launchpad

Let's paint a picture. Imagine Sarah and Ben, drowning in a $1,200 monthly rent payment for an apartment they'll never own. It feels like setting money on fire. They take a leap. They work with family, pool resources, and build a stylish, functional ADU in a relative's backyard for $40,000. Poof! That $1,200 rent vanishes. Suddenly, that money isn't just gone; it's actively paying off their own little haven. In less than three years, purely from the rent they stopped paying, their investment is covered. Everything after that? Pure financial oxygen. Maybe it fuels that backpacking trip they always dreamed of, seeds a small business, or simply buys them the priceless commodity of peace of mind. This isn't just a daydream; real people are making this happen, especially as communities wake up and adopt ADU-friendly rules (hat tip to places like California leading the charge, as tracked by folks like UC Berkeley's Terner Center).

More Than Just Savings: A Swiss Army Knife of Solutions

But the beauty of micro-living goes way beyond the bank account. These small spaces are incredibly versatile:

Keeping Family Close: They offer dignified, independent living for aging parents right in the backyard – closeness without being too close (something groups like AARP champion).

Smart Income Streams: Renting out an ADU can be a brilliant "house hack," helping homeowners tackle their own mortgage payments.

Creative Sanctuaries: They become dream home offices, sun-drenched art studios, or welcoming guest suites, adding layers of function and joy to a property without the cost of a massive extension.

Treading Lighter: Let's face it, smaller homes are just kinder to our planet. They demand fewer materials to build and sip energy for heating and cooling instead of guzzling it, shrinking our carbon footprint day by day (data from the U.S. Energy Information Administration confirms this!).

The Big Idea in a Small Package

The micro-home movement, in all its tiny house and ADU glory, is more than just a trend; it's a fundamental rethinking of "home." It challenges us to question how much space we really need to live well. It's a compelling invitation to trade excess square footage for financial freedom, adaptability, deeper connections, and a gentler impact on the earth.

It's proof that sometimes, the most profound wins come from living just a little bit smaller.

Okay, let's ditch the dry stats for a sec and talk about that gut-punch feeling when the utility bill lands. You know the one. It sits there, maybe on the kitchen counter, radiating a low-key dread. It feels like this relentless opponent, always winning, always taking a bigger bite out of your hard-earned cash.

But what if you could change the game? What if you could learn a little "Utility Judo"? Forget shivering in a single sweater or taking navy showers. This isn't about deprivation; it's about being clever. It's about using the weight of those energy costs against themselves, turning that financial drain into a trickle, and eventually, maybe even a source of savings flowing back to you.

Think about it: where does most of that energy money go? Keeping our homes cozy – warm in the winter, cool in the summer. That heating and cooling system is often the biggest energy hog in the house, gobbling up nearly half our energy use, according to the folks who track this stuff (like the DOE). That makes it ground zero for our Utility Judo moves.

Now, let's zoom in on another thirsty contender: the water heater. Whether it's for showers, dishes, or laundry, heating water quietly sucks down a significant chunk of energy – often the second or third biggest expense on that bill (think 14-18%, says ENERGY STAR). It's a constant, background drain.

Here's where a seriously slick Judo move comes in: harnessing the sun. Imagine tapping into that giant, free fusion reactor hanging 93 million miles away to heat your water. A solar water heater does exactly that. It feels almost like cheating, doesn't it? Using sunshine instead of paying for gas or electricity.

Now, let's be real – installing one isn't free. While someone might mention a $400 figure linked to savings (maybe that's a super-specific rebate or just one part?), the actual upfront cost to get a system on your roof usually ranges from a few thousand to ten thousand dollars, depending on your home, location, and the system itself (NREL data confirms this). But, and this is the crucial Judo flip, think long-term. Agencies like the DOE point out these systems can slash your water heating costs by half or even more. That $70 monthly savings mentioned in the example? That's $840 a year staying in your pocket, not going to the utility company. Year after year. Suddenly, that upfront cost starts looking less like an expense and more like a savvy investment, paying you back over its long lifespan (often 20+ years!). Add in tax credits and local incentives (check resources like DSIRE!), and the math gets even better.

Picture the Millers again. Instead of just "grappling," imagine them tired of that monthly budget rollercoaster, always bracing for the utility bill spike. They take the plunge, make the investment in solar water heating. That first bill arrives after installation... and there's a noticeable dip. It's not just numbers; it's a feeling of relief, of having outsmarted the system. Month after month, that $70 (or whatever their actual saving is) feels like reclaiming territory. Over the years, it's not just savings; it's financial breathing room, money freed up for other things. They didn't just cut an expense; they flipped it.

And this isn't just a homeowner's game. Think about a local laundromat, constantly churning through hot water, or a bustling restaurant kitchen. For them, hot water isn't just comfort; it's essential overhead. A commercial-scale solar water heating system can be a game-changer, turning a major operating cost into a much smaller one, boosting their bottom line (NREL research backs this up). Even communities are getting in on the act, setting up shared solar systems so folks who can't put panels on their own roof can still benefit. And don't worry if you're not living in perpetual sunshine; modern systems are surprisingly effective even in less sunny regions (thanks to tech advancements tracked by groups like the IEA).

Ultimately, Utility Judo is a mindset shift. It's looking at that energy bill not as an unbeatable foe, but as an opportunity. It's realizing that smart upgrades, like harnessing the sun for your hot water, aren't just spending money – they're strategic investments designed to pay you back, again and again. It's about doing the research, understanding the real costs and potential savings, grabbing those incentives, and executing the flip – turning the pressure of high bills into the sweet relief of ongoing savings. Now that's a winning move.

Food Security—Eating Well on Less

Dancing with the Seasons: How Your Grocery Cart Can Groove to Nature's Beat (and Save You Cash)

Ever get that ouch feeling staring at a tiny box of berries in January, priced like precious jewels? Or feel like you're practically stealing pumpkins come Halloween? That's not random market madness; it's the quiet whisper of the seasons, a rhythm you can learn to dance to, turning your grocery runs into a savvy shuffle that saves you real money. Think of it less like budgeting, more like having a secret handshake with Mother Nature, one that pads your wallet just by paying attention.

So, what's the secret sauce? It's simpler than you think, something economists wrap in fancy terms like "supply and demand," but really, it's just common sense grown wild. When the sun's high and the soil's happy, local fields explode with life – tomatoes blush on the vine, zucchini practically multiplies overnight. Nature throws a giant, delicious party, and suddenly, there's so much amazing food around. Farms are overflowing, markets are bustling, and prices? They naturally take a dip. It's a buyer's paradise!

Flip the calendar. Craving that crisp asparagus when snow's on the ground (in many spots, anyway)? That spear likely wasn't lounging in a nearby field. It might have journeyed thousands of miles, snuggled in a climate-controlled container, or grown under expensive artificial suns. All that special treatment – the travel, the cozy storage, the high-tech farming – adds up, and you see it reflected in that heftier price tag. It's the difference between grabbing abundance from your doorstep versus commissioning a special delivery from afar.

And the savings aren't just a few cents here and there. We're talking about a potential windfall. Imagine slashing your fruit-and-veg spend significantly! Research backs this up – a deep dive by the USDA in 2024 found that folks syncing their shopping with peak harvest times could pocket savings averaging up to 45% compared to buying those same items when they're playing hard to get. That's not just pocket change; that's potentially freeing up serious cash for other things you love. It's a well-documented groove: when the harvest peaks, prices tend to hit their lowest notes.

Picture this: Sarah, who rings you up at the local market, needs winter squash for her famous soup. In the heart of autumn, gorgeous golden globes – butternut, acorn, spaghetti – are piled high, practically glowing. They're fresh off the vine, maybe from a farm just down the road, and she bags them for about $1 a pound. Fast forward to late spring. She spots that same type of squash, looking a bit weary from its long journey or storage, now demanding $2.50 per pound. Yikes! That's a 150% jump! By leaning into squash season when it's truly squash season, Sarah saved herself $1.50 on every pound – a cool 60% off, just by timing it right. That USDA number suddenly feels very real, doesn't it?

Now, imagine weaving this rhythm into your family's meals. Summer kitchens filled with the scent of bursting berries, sun-warmed tomatoes, and endless zucchini creations. Hitting the farmers' market feels like finding treasure, getting the freshest stuff directly from the folks who grew it, often at prices that make you smile. Then, as leaves turn golden, the menu shifts – crisp apples, earthy root veggies begging to be roasted, hearty greens like kale taking center stage. It's a delicious cycle! By consciously flowing with what's abundant, families can tap into those significant savings year-round. Even fancy restaurants get it; those "seasonal specials" aren't just clever marketing – they're often the chef's nod to what's currently best, freshest, and most affordable, a smart move for flavor and the bottom line.

But here's the beautiful bonus: tuning into the seasons isn't just about the dollars. It's about taste. Food eaten at its peak, ripened naturally, just tastes better. That July tomato has a sweetness a January import can only dream of. That autumn apple has a snap that speaks of crisp air and sunshine. Food science often confirms what our taste buds know: peak season means peak flavor. Plus, choosing local and seasonal often means your food hasn't clocked up as many "food miles," a gentle nod towards a lighter footprint on our planet.

So, next time you're mapping out your meals or wandering the produce aisle, pause for a second. Listen. What is nature offering right now? Leaning into that abundance isn't just frugal; it's flowing with a natural, delicious, and economically sound current. It's a simple shift, a way to let the earth's own rhythms trim your bills and thrill your palate. Give it a try – your wallet (and your taste buds) might just sing your praises.

Okay, let's ditch the formal talk and get real about those grocery bills that seem to have sprouted legs and run sky-high. Feeling like your wallet weeps every time you hit the checkout? Yeah, me too. But what if we could fight back, not with coupons alone, but with a bit of delicious, old-school kitchen wizardry? Forget dusty cookbooks – let's talk about turning your kitchen into a time machine for flavor and savings through freezing and canning.

Think of it like this: you're becoming a savvy investor, but instead of stocks, you're dealing in sunshine-ripened tomatoes and crisp autumn apples. The market's flooded in summer? Prices plummet. That's your signal! You swoop in, grab those gorgeous fruits and veggies (or that bulk buy of chicken) when they're practically giving them away, and then? Magic. You use the superpowers of your freezer or the alchemy of canning jars to lock that peak freshness and rock-bottom price away for a rainy (or snowy, or just plain expensive) day. It's about capturing abundance, bottling sunshine, and telling future-you, "Hey, I got you covered." Forget boring percentages; imagine slashing a chunk off your winter grocery spending because your freezer is already bursting with summer berries you bought for a song.

Let's start with the freezer – your cool, quiet partner in preservation crime. This is gateway magic, folks. Super easy. Got berries threatening to turn mushy? A bounty of bell peppers from the market? Bananas looking a tad too brown for breakfast but perfect for smoothies? Wash, chop (maybe a quick blanch for some veggies – like a mini spa treatment!), and into the cold they go. Picture Sarah, staring down a mountain of June strawberries she snagged for a steal. A little effort now – washing, hulling, freezing flat – means come January, when a tiny plastic box of berries costs more than her fancy coffee, she's whipping up vibrant smoothies and desserts, smugly knowing she saved a bundle. Plus, freezing is like hitting the pause button on nutrients; that frosty nap locks in the good stuff, sometimes even better than veggies that have journeyed for days to reach the shelf.

Ready for level two? Canning. Okay, it asks for a bit more commitment – jars, lids, maybe a big pot (canner). But oh, the treasures it yields! This is where you transform humble cucumbers into snappy pickles, overflowing tomatoes into jars of rich, ruby sauce, and summer peaches into golden preserves that taste like pure sunshine on toast. It's a process, sure – heating things just right to keep them safe and shelf-stable for ages, sealing out the spoilers. Think of community gardens drowning in zucchini – neighbours gather, chop, simmer, and seal, turning potential waste into rows of gleaming jars, a shared pantry of homemade goodness that laughs in the face of store-bought prices. Safety's key here, especially with less acidic foods (listen to the experts like the NCHFP!), but the payoff is a pantry that feels like a personal Fort Knox of flavour.

But here's the real beauty: this isn't just about saving cash (though, hello, major perk!). It's a quiet rebellion against waste. How much perfectly good food sadly wilts in our fridges? Preservation gives it a second life! It's about knowing exactly what's in your food – you're the boss of the salt, the sugar, the spices. No mystery ingredients here. And honestly? There's a deep, almost primal satisfaction in lining up jars you filled yourself, or pulling a bag of frozen summer goodness from the depths of your freezer. It's tangible proof of your cleverness, your care, your delicious defiance.

So, whether you're freezing a few bags of seasonal bounty or diving deep into the bubbling pots of canning, you're doing more than just trimming the budget. You're weaving resourcefulness into your routine, rescuing food, taking control of your ingredients, and ensuring that the taste of peak season can brighten even the greyest day. In times like these, knowing how to stretch, save, and savor isn't just smart; it feels downright powerful.

Tired of That Grocery Store Gut Punch? Let's Flip the Script, Neighbor-Style.

You know that feeling, right? You're wandering the aisles, grabbing the basics – rice, flour, maybe some beans – and every beep at the checkout feels like a tiny little heist on your wallet. Prices just keep climbing, like they've got little rocket boosters strapped to them.

But what if I told you there's a kind of neighborhood superpower hiding in plain sight? Imagine this: you, Sarah from down the block, maybe Dave from across the street, all deciding, "Enough!" You pool your grocery lists, not just your wish lists, but the real lists – the sacks of staples that keep your kitchens running.

This isn't some complicated scheme; it's a Co-op Collective, a fancy term for something beautifully simple: neighbors becoming shopping buddies on a bigger scale. Think of it as a secret handshake for saving money. Instead of each of you buying a small, pricey bag of oats, you team up. Suddenly, you're not just a handful of shoppers; you're a force. You can walk straight past the retail shelves (metaphorically speaking, mostly!) and knock on the doors of wholesalers, distributors, maybe even local farms. You buy in bulk – think giant sacks, cases, the whole shebang – and unlock prices that make those supermarket tags look almost comical.

It's Not Just Pennies, It's Real Dough (Pun Intended!)

Seriously, the savings are legit. When you band together, suppliers see a bigger, juicier order and are way more willing to cut you a deal. Forget loyalty cards; collective buying is the real discount code. Experts (the folks who study this stuff, like at the National Grocers Association) found that people doing this kind of cooperative buying were saving around 22% on average compared to regular retail prices. That's like getting every fifth bag of groceries free!

Why? Because you're cutting out the fluff. No fancy store rent in a prime location, no splashy ad campaigns, no layers upon layers of middlemen adding their cut. It's just you, your neighbors, and a more direct line to the source.

Picture this: That bag of rice costing you $1.20 a pound at the store? Your little neighborhood crew might snag a massive 50-pound sack directly from a supplier, bringing the cost down to maybe $0.80 a pound. Boom! That's 40 cents saved on every single pound. If five families just like yours use, say, 125 pounds of rice a year each (that's 625 pounds total), your little group just saved $250 together ($50 per family!)... just on rice. Now, multiply that magic across flour, pasta, lentils, oats, cooking oil, heck, even toilet paper or soap! It adds up fast, creating a welcome cushion against those ever-rising costs. It's the simple power of buying big – less packaging waste per pound, lower shipping costs per item, pure economic sense.

So, How Does This Neighborhood Magic Actually Work?

It can look a few different ways, fitting whatever vibe your street has:

The Back Pocket Brigade: Maybe it starts super casual. Just you and a couple of immediate neighbors. Someone finds a good deal at a Costco Business Center or a local farm distributor. You sling messages back and forth on a group chat, Venmo the organizer, and divvy up the haul from someone's garage or porch. It runs on trust and knowing who needs five pounds of pinto beans this month. Simple, fast, effective.

The Community Club: A bit more organized, maybe covering a wider neighborhood chunk. You might have a dedicated organizer (or rotate the job), a regular monthly or quarterly order cycle focusing on dry goods or even shares of local produce. There's a set pickup spot and time. Think of it like a potluck, but for stocking your pantry smarter.

The Digital Handshake: Tech can lend a hand, too. Some apps or online platforms are popping up specifically to connect neighbors and streamline group orders from local suppliers. They handle the tricky bits of collecting money and coordinating, but the heart of it is still neighbors pooling their power.

The Pre-Order Pros: These groups often skip a physical 'store' entirely. Everyone decides what they want, pays upfront, and the order gets delivered to one central spot for pickup. It's super efficient, cuts down on waste (no guessing what people might buy), and those savings flow right back to you.

More Than Just Groceries: It's Community Currency

Honestly, joining forces like this does more than just save cash (though that part is really nice). It's about reconnecting with the people right next door. It's about sharing tips, maybe splitting that enormous bag of lentils, and knowing you're all in it together. It turns a chore – grocery shopping – into a shared victory.

It's a practical, powerful way to build resilience right on your street, proving that sometimes the best solutions are found not on a distant corporate spreadsheet, but in the simple act of neighbors helping neighbors. One bulk bag of awesome at a time.

Subtopic 4: Your Concrete Jungle Oasis: Finding Flavor (and Savings) Where You Least Expect It

Feel that disconnect? That little pang when you eye the wilting herbs in the plastic box, knowing half will go bad before you use them? Or maybe it's the ever-climbing grocery bill whispering anxieties in your ear as you navigate the fluorescent aisles. City life is vibrant, electric, but it can also sever our roots to where our food really comes from, leaving us feeling like passive consumers rather than participants. And space? Forget about it. A sprawling garden seems like a fairytale when your reality is measured in square feet, not acres.

But hold that thought. Glance at that patch of sunlight spilling onto your windowsill, that sliver of a balcony that mostly holds a dusty chair, that quiet corner of the patio. Think they're just dead space? Think again. These aren't limitations; they're invitations. They're blank canvases whispering possibilities. Welcome to the quiet revolution sprouting in the heart of the city: Urban Harvest. It's not about replicating a farm; it's about coaxing life, flavour, and yes, even a little bit of financial breathing room, from the most unexpected urban pockets. It starts with a simple, delicious goal: making your grocery money stretch further by growing something yourself.

Forget complex spreadsheets for a moment. We're talking about the simple, satisfying math of snipping your own basil – fragrant, alive, bursting with flavour – instead of buying another $4 bunch destined for the crisper drawer graveyard. Does it really add up? You bet. Folks are finding that even a few well-loved pots can shave a couple of hundred dollars off their yearly food spend. Think about those high-ticket items: the delicate herbs, the crisp salad greens that wilt too soon, the jewel-like tomatoes or vibrant peppers that cost a premium, especially when you crave them mid-winter or want the organic promise. These are the heroes of the small-space garden, the ones that give back generously. It's not just wishful thinking; careful gardeners and even number-crunching university programs agree – growing even some of your own, especially these quick-turnaround, pricey goodies, puts real money back in your pocket, even after you've bought the pot and soil.

Let's paint a picture: Imagine Sarah, a teacher whose only 'outdoor' space is a balcony barely big enough for two chairs. Last summer, she decided to try her hand at cherry tomatoes and a pot of unstoppable basil. By summer's end, she wasn't just enjoying sun-warmed tomatoes in her salads and fragrant basil on her pasta; she realized she'd skipped buying those items entirely for months, saving herself around $80. It wasn't about feeding herself solely from the balcony; it was smart, tasty substitution. Why pay for convenience when you can cultivate joy (and savings)? The math sings loudest for these perishable treasures – the faster they grow and the more they cost at the store, the quicker your little green investment pays delicious dividends.

But this story unfolds beyond just one balcony. Picture this: Your kitchen window, no longer just a view, but a living pantry. Imagine window boxes spilling over with a riot of lettuce greens – spicy arugula, tender butterhead, vibrant red oakleaf. You're not just growing salad; you're crafting your perfect mix, snipping what you need moments before dinner, ditching the plastic bags and the wilting disappointment. Or think bigger, even in small ways. Imagine those forgotten strips of city soil, those lonely patches beside sidewalks, transformed by neighbours into shared herb havens, a fragrant library where everyone can 'check out' a sprig of rosemary or thyme, sharing the bounty and the savings.

Got only a whisper of floor space? Look up! Vertical gardens are scaling walls, turning blank surfaces into cascading tapestries of sweet strawberries, diverse lettuces, and essential herbs. It's like discovering extra square footage you never knew you had, dedicated purely to deliciousness and shrinking those grocery receipts. The upfront cost? Often recouped faster than you'd think, transforming a patch of wall into a source of fresh, free flavour.

The most beautiful part? This isn't some exclusive club. It doesn't demand a sprawling estate or a degree in horticulture. It asks for a splash of sunlight, a container (get creative – old buckets, cracked mugs, repurposed tins can find new life!), some decent soil, a packet of seeds or a little starter plant, and a spark of curiosity. The journey might start with the satisfying crunch of saving money, watching those grocery bills shrink. But soon, you discover the other treasures: the unparalleled taste of a tomato still warm from the sun, the quiet joy of watching a tiny seed bravely push through the soil, the grounding connection to the rhythm of nature, right there amidst the city buzz. It's about more than just food; it's about reclaiming a little piece of the earth, finding freshness in unexpected corners, and tasting the sweet, simple satisfaction of saying, "I grew this myself."

Income Amplifiers–Side Hustles That Stick

Okay, let's ditch the boardroom speak and talk about you. You know all that stuff rattling around in your head? The skills you've picked up like shiny pebbles on the beach – from your day job, your weekend obsessions, even just figuring out how to adult successfully? That's not just random knowledge. It's potential cash, waiting to be unleashed.

Think about it. That thing you do effortlessly, the one people always ask you about? Maybe it's untangling spreadsheet chaos, writing emails that actually get opened, charming grumpy customers, knowing exactly how to prune a rose bush, or having an encyclopedic knowledge of 80s synth-pop? To you, it might feel like breathing. To someone else? It's a superpower they'd happily pay for.

This isn't some far-fetched dream anymore. We're living in an age where your unique brand of awesome can find its audience, its paying audience, often without you even leaving your couch. Forget dusty old notions of "work." The freelance world is buzzing, a massive global marketplace hungry for exactly the kind of smarts you possess. Seriously, look around – tons of people are ditching the traditional grind, or at least adding a lucrative side-stage, powered by their own expertise. It's a full-blown movement.

Let's Talk Treasure (Real Money!)

Okay, does it pay? You bet. While "average" freelance rates float around (think maybe $30 an hour, according to the stat folks in 2024), "average" is kinda boring, right? Your specific magic – that niche skill, your years of experience, how brilliantly you solve someone's headache – that dictates your real value. Tech wizards and creative dynamos can command way more, while helping someone organize their digital life might pay differently. The point is: it's real money, earned on your terms, using the brilliance you already have.

But it's often about more than just stacking coins. This is about adding flex to your finances, maybe building that "uh-oh" fund, fueling that passion project you keep dreaming about, or just experiencing the sheer thrill of getting paid for being you. There's a spark, a sense of control and satisfaction that comes from knowing your skills are valuable out there in the wild.

From "Just Doing My Job" to "Getting Paid Extra For My Genius"

Remember that receptionist example? Let's call her Sarah. Sarah wasn't just answering phones; she was a communication ninja, an organizational guru, maybe even the secret weapon behind killer internal memos. She realized, "Hey, businesses need blogs, and I know how to string words together clearly." Boom. A few hours a week tapping into that existing skill, and suddenly there's an extra $400 rolling in. That's not life-altering wealth, maybe, but it's meaningful cash flow conjured from her everyday toolkit. That's the alchemy we're talking about.

Or picture the graphic designer, brilliant but maybe a bit bored designing corporate brochures. On their own time? They become a brand whisperer for startups, crafting logos that pop, social media graphics that sizzle. They're taking their core professional superpower and unleashing it in a more exciting, potentially much more lucrative, playground.

Think about the patient math teacher. Beyond the classroom walls, their ability to make numbers click is pure gold. Online tutoring platforms become their stage, connecting them with students craving that 'aha!' moment. They're literally cashing in on their knowledge and teaching heart, tapping into a huge demand for personalized learning.

Even that neighbour obsessed with their award-winning tomatoes and compost bin? That's not just a hobby; it's expertise! They could launch a paid newsletter spilling their secrets, host online workshops on sustainable gardening, or offer virtual garden consultations. They're turning their passion, their earthy wisdom, into streams of income, proving that anything you know deeply can be valuable.

Unlock Your Inner Freelancer

So, what's your secret sauce? What do you know, do, or love that someone else might need? Monetizing your skills through freelancing is about looking at yourself through a fresh lens. It takes a moment of honesty ("What am I genuinely good at?"), a dash of detective work ("Who needs this? Where are they?"), and the courage to step onto the digital stage.

Whether it's skills honed over a long career, knowledge packed away during your studies, or talents nurtured in your downtime – the opportunity to turn what you know into tangible reward has never been more real or exciting. Your unique brilliance is waiting for its spotlight. Go find it.

Planting Digital Seeds: How Your Quirks Can Blossom into Cash

Imagine that thing you just know? That knack you have? Maybe it's how you tame your wild spreadsheet chaos, the secret sauce to your sourdough starter, or the way you make tiny apartment balconies burst with life. Now, picture bottling that spark – not in glass, but in pixels – and setting it free online.

This isn't about building some colossal digital empire overnight. Nope. This is about micro-creation: crafting tiny, helpful digital treasures from your unique brainwaves. Think handy templates that save someone hours, checklists that cut through confusion, presets that make photos pop, or simple guides that unlock a skill. You pour your magic into it once, and like a little digital seed, it can sprout into sales again and again, even while you're dreaming about your next big idea (or just, you know, actually sleeping).

Why does this feel so right, right now? Because the old ways – warehouses groaning with stuff, complicated shipping, needing a dragon's hoard of gold to start – just don't apply here. Your workshop is your mind, your tools are likely already on your computer, and your inventory is... infinite. It throws open the doors for anyone with a specific passion or a clever solution to share it and earn from it. Forget fitting into a neat job title; this is about carving out your own little niche in the world. And guess what? People are hungry for these shortcuts, these elegant solutions. They'll happily trade a few bucks for something that solves a nagging problem or saves them precious time. The digital world is buzzing with folks looking for exactly what you might have to offer (just ask the trend-watchers at places like Statista – they see this digital market growing like a weed!).

Does it actually work? Ask the folks quietly succeeding on platforms like Gumroad. While nobody waves a magic wand guaranteeing "$X per month," the whispers in creator circles and the buzz online tell a consistent story: small, focused products can build real momentum. That

$10 template? Find 60 people who need it this month – maybe through your blog, your tiny Instagram following, or a niche community – and suddenly, that's $600. It's not about hitting the jackpot overnight; it's about connecting your specific solution with the specific people searching for it, one sale at a time.

Let's make it real:

The Balcony Whisperer: You know Sarah? She's got an almost magical touch with container gardening on her tiny city balcony. Beginners kept asking her the same questions. Instead of endless DMs, she poured her wisdom into "The Balcony Bloom Kit" – printable planners, a no-fail veggie guide for pots, and her secret weapon checklist against pesky bugs. She sells it for $15 on her small blog. Twenty sales a month? That's $300 earned from sharing what she loves, validating her green thumb while she plans her next planting season. It's pure, passion-fueled passive income.

The Notion Navigator: Alex lives and breathes Notion, turning digital chaos into sleek, organized dashboards. They saw freelancers drowning in admin. Solution? They built the "Freelancer Freedom Hub" template – tracking projects, clients, invoices, goals, all in one elegant package for $49. Too much for some? Okay, how about a simple "Spark Content Calendar" template for just $9? By solving the overwhelm for Notion users (a huge, eager crowd!), Alex is building a thriving little digital shop, fueled by rave reviews in productivity forums.

The Canva Wizard: Meet Chloe, a designer who realized small businesses desperately need decent social media graphics but often lack the budget or skills. She started creating packs of gorgeous, editable Canva templates – chic designs for cafes, sharp layouts for real estate agents, calming visuals for wellness coaches. A pack of 20 templates goes for $25. Suddenly, those small biz owners look polished online, and Chloe's leveraging her design skills far beyond one-on-one gigs. Etsy is brimming with stories like hers, where digital downloads are a vibrant part of the creative economy.

Micro-creation is about translating that unique spark inside you into a digital helping hand for someone else. It starts with spotting that little frustration, that gap in knowledge, that wish for a shortcut. You craft your elegant little solution, find its home online, and let it find its way to the people who need it. Yes, it takes heart and effort upfront, and you'll need to let people know it exists. But the beauty? That little digital seed, once planted, can keep blossoming long after you've moved on to nurturing the next idea. What tiny treasure are you waiting to share?

Rewritten Content: Your Street, Your Superstore: The Magic of Neighborly Commerce

Forget the anonymous clicks that send your cash continents away for a moment. Lean in closer. Listen. There's a quiet hum, a different kind of economy waking up right outside your door. It's the magic of local exchange, and it's simpler and more powerful than you might think. It's about seeing your street, your block, your neighborhood not just as rows of houses, but as a vibrant marketplace brimming with hidden talents and surprising treasures.

Think about it: that neighbor down the street who bakes bread that makes your soul sing? The teenager next door who's a wizard with cranky computers? The retiree with the green thumb coaxing miracles out of their backyard plot? This isn't just about convenience, though that's part of it. It's a conscious choice to weave our resources – our skills, our time, our money – directly into the fabric of the place we call home. It's looking across the fence, not across the country, and realizing the value is right here.

Sure, you might hear about online crafters pulling in $500 a month (and good on them!), but that's just one thread in a much richer tapestry. The real story unfolds in countless ways, often quietly, organically. It's the neighborly "gig economy," where passions turn into pocket money, and needs find solutions just steps away. Studies whisper about a potent "local multiplier effect"—how even a small shift in spending towards the folks down the road can make our shared community noticeably richer, circulating value instead of siphoning it away. Farmers' markets buzz with this energy, proving we crave that connection to where our goods come from, pouring billions back into local soil. It's commerce with a handshake, a story, a familiar face.

Let's paint a picture beyond just crafty candles:

The Aroma of Opportunity: Imagine Sarah, mastering the art of sourdough under cottage food laws. Her kitchen isn't just a kitchen; it's a micro-bakery. Through a neighborhood Facebook group and the power of scent wafting down the street, she sells loaves and decorated cookies – maybe earning $400, maybe $700 a month. It's income for her, yes, but it's also real, fresh bread for her neighbors, the kind you can't find shrink-wrapped. She's not just baking; she's building a tastier community, one crusty loaf at a time.

The Local Tech Lifeline: Remember Ron, the retired IT guru? Instead of navigating faceless corporate support lines, neighbors call Ron. He sets up shop (metaphorically!) via Nextdoor or a flyer at the local library, untangling Wi-Fi woes and demystifying software updates, maybe adding a few hundred dollars to his retirement fund. He's not just fixing computers; he's bridging the digital divide with patience and a familiar smile, keeping tech stress hyper-local and manageable.

The Veggie Vine: Think Community Supported Agriculture (CSA), but with a neighborhood twist. Maybe Dave doesn't farm, but his porch becomes the weekly pickup point for 12 families getting fresh produce directly from Farmer McGregor just outside town. Dave's role is simple – being the friendly hub – but it strengthens the chain, connects families to their food source, and gives the farmer predictable income. He's a vital knot in the local food web.

The Neighborhood Mender: Meet Maria, the person you call when the faucet won't stop dripping, the flat-pack furniture looks like a puzzle from Hades, or the wall has an unfortunate encounter with a doorknob. She's the 'fixer,' helping busy parents and elderly residents through word-of-mouth, perhaps earning $500-$800 monthly. She's not just patching holes; she's mending the daily frustrations of life, providing peace of mind and reliable help right where it's needed.

This is what local exchange feels like. It turns streets into ecosystems of skill and need. It sparks conversations over garden gates, builds trust transaction by transaction, and shortens the journey from maker to user, leaving a lighter footprint on the planet. It keeps the lifeblood – the money, the energy, the connection – circulating right here, making our neighborhoods not just places to live, but places that thrive. It's about recognizing the wealth isn't miles away; it's in the skills, passions, and helping hands right next door. It's truly trading up our communities, from the inside out.

Turning Dead Time into Dollars: Your Pocket-Sized Power-Up

You know that feeling? The calendar page flips, a surprise bill lands like a rogue ninja star, or maybe you're just dreaming of swapping your routine for a beach chair for a few days. In the old grind, finding quick cash felt like squeezing water from a stone. But guess what? Your phone, that thing glued to your hand? It's not just for scrolling – it's a potential ATM.

Welcome to the magic of gig flexibility. It's about grabbing those random pockets of time – that sleepy Saturday morning, those couple of hours after dinner – and turning them into actual money. No soul-crushing commute to a second job, no begging for overtime. Just you, your skills (or your car!), an app, and the open road (literal or digital).

Why does this feel so good? One word: Control. Forget rigid schedules. You punch the clock when you want. Feel like working Tuesday night but sleeping in Wednesday? Go for it. Need to make bank this weekend but lay low next? You're the captain now. Study after study whispers the same secret: people crave this freedom, this power to say "yes" or "no" to work based on their life, not a pre-set timetable. It's how you juggle kids, classes, passion projects, or just, you know, life.

Now, let's talk cash, because "Big Returns" sounds nice, but what does it mean? Okay, maybe you hear figures like $15 an hour driving for Uber (remember, that's before gas, wear-and-tear, etc. – keep it real!). But think about it: sacrifice 10 hours of scrolling or channel-surfing on a weekend, and boom – potentially $150 (before costs) closer to paying that bill or funding that getaway. It might not replace a full-time salary overnight, but financial gurus have seen it happen again and again: this kind of income acts like a shock absorber for your budget, smoothing out those scary financial bumps.

And it's not just driving! This idea bursts into life in so many ways:

The Weekend Side-Quest: Think of the office clerk who transforms into a weekend driver. That extra $300 they pocket isn't just random cash; it's the car payment vanishing, a down payment fund growing, or simply the sweet relief of a less-stressed budget. They've given those earnings a job.

The Campus Hustler: Picture the student squeezing in food deliveries between Econ 101 and Chemistry lab. Those few hours translate into cash for textbooks, late-night pizza, or just easing the reliance on loans. It's freedom fuel, earned on their own quirky schedule.

The After-Hours Artisan: Imagine the graphic designer, already working a 9-to-5, logging into a freelance platform at night. They knock out a quick logo design or a social media banner. It's not just extra money; it's using their superpowers for targeted strikes – maybe funding better software or that industry conference.

The Task Tackler: See the person spending a Saturday afternoon assembling someone's nightmare flat-pack furniture via an app like TaskRabbit. They're leveraging pure elbow grease and practicality for instant cash. Need beer money tonight? Assemble that bookshelf!

Ultimately, gig work, in these short bursts, is about agility. It's your financial multi-tool. It lets you mold your free time around your money needs, not the other way around. While you always need to factor in the real costs and know it fluctuates, the sheer power to generate a few hundred extra bucks, just when you need it, using the tech already in your pocket? That's a seriously valuable superpower in today's world. It's transforming idle moments into empowered action.

Mobility on a Budget—Transportation That Works

Forget the Awkward Silence: Carpooling Just Got Cool Again

Whisper the word "carpool" and what springs to mind? Maybe fuzzy memories of your parents coordinating schedules over landlines, juggling juice boxes and briefcases, or those slightly stiff rides home from work where the radio station was always a battleground? For a while there, carpooling felt like a relic, a dusty concept parked in the garage of Good Ideas We Don't Quite Do Anymore.

But hold up. Feel that? There's a new vibe on the streets. Carpooling is back, not as a creaky throwback, but as a sleek, savvy, digitally-powered movement. It's less about faded sign-up sheets tacked to a corkboard and more about tapping into a dynamic network humming right inside your phone. This isn't your grandma's ride-share; it's carpooling reimagined.

So, what lit the fuse for this comeback? Let's be real: our wallets are screaming. Every time that gas pump clicks higher, the idea of splitting the cost feels less like a chore and more like a financial superpower. Add a dash of eco-awareness – that growing nudge telling us our solo drives might be choking the planet – and the plot thickens. Then there's the soul-crushing reality of traffic. You know, that daily bumper-to-bumper ballet where minutes stretch into eternities? Gliding past it all in an HOV lane suddenly feels like unlocking a secret level in the game of commuting. It's not just a hunch; transportation gurus confirm that fewer lone drivers mean less gridlock and more precious time rescued from the asphalt jungle.

But the real magic, the secret sauce turning this old concept into a modern marvel, is technology. Think of it as a digital cupid for your commute. Slick apps and platforms are playing matchmaker, using smart algorithms to pair drivers and riders heading the same way, sometimes even on the fly. Forget awkward IOUs; integrated payments make splitting costs smoother than a fresh pour of coffee. Worried about riding with a stranger? User ratings and profiles build a web of trust. Need to coordinate pickup? GPS tracking keeps everyone in the loop. It's this tech infusion that vaporizes the old logistical headaches, making finding a ride-buddy easier than finding your keys (most days).

And the cash savings? They're not pocket change. Imagine slicing potentially 40% off your fuel bill – that's the kind of number environmental brainiacs toss around when talking about cutting down vehicle miles. It's simple math backed by energy experts: drive less (by sharing more), save more. Real money, back in your pocket.

Look around, it's already happening:

The Commuter Lifeline: Picture Maya, a healthcare hero whose long drive to the hospital was draining her energy and her bank account ($150+ a month just on gas!). A quick sign-up on her workplace ride-share board connected her with a fellow healer down the street. Now, they swap driving days, slashing costs, easing car maintenance, and maybe even swapping stories from the front lines. Experts say consistent carpoolers like Maya can pocket thousands saved each year.

Corporate Karma: Over at that shiny tech campus, they're not just coding the future; they're driving it smarter. To hit green goals and solve the parking puzzle, the company dangles prime parking spots for employees who team up for the commute. Internal tools, often synced with popular apps, make finding ride-matches within the company a breeze. It's proof that a little incentive goes a long way.

Campus Cruisers: University life often means battling for pricey, elusive parking spots. Students, masters of the hustle, are ditching the solo drive and hopping into shared rides found via campus-specific or general carpool apps. It's budget-friendly, parking-permit-panic-reducing, and hey, maybe you make a new study buddy.

Event Escapes: Heading to that big game or concert? Instead of bracing for ride-hail surge pricing or shelling out for stadium parking that costs more than your ticket, people are using dedicated app features or platforms to find fellow fans heading the same way. It cuts costs, slashes venue traffic jams, and starts the fun before you even arrive.

This carpooling renaissance is about more than just saving dough or shrinking our carbon tyre-print (though those are huge wins). It's about using the smartest tools we have to bring back a fundamentally smart way to travel. It's about reclaiming stolen hours from traffic jams, dialing down the daily stress, and maybe, just maybe, sparking a little human connection in the space between Point A and Point B. Sure, matching schedules and building that initial trust still takes a little effort, but by blending an age-old idea with today's tech, modern carpooling isn't just practical – it feels like the future. Ready to share the ride?

Okay, let's ditch the spreadsheets and the dry stats for a moment. Think of your city's buses and trains not just as ways to get from A to B, but as your secret weapon for a richer life – and yes, I mean richer in your wallet and maybe even your mood. We're talking about becoming a Transit Ninja, mastering the art of public transport to slash those pesky expenses that drain your bank account faster than a leaky faucet.

Forget the idea that public transit is just a backup plan. It's time to see it as Plan A+ for your finances.

Your Car: The Sneaky Money Vampire

Let's be real. Owning a car feels like freedom, right? Until the bills roll in. It's not just the loan payment or the eye-watering insurance premium. It's the gas station visits that feel like highway robbery, the oil changes, the new tires, that weird clunking sound that turns into a four-figure repair bill, the parking meters gobbling your change, the tolls... it's a relentless financial assault! Experts toss around figures, like saving maybe $700 a year on average by switching (thanks, APTA!), but honestly? That often feels like the tip of the iceberg. Dig deeper, and you find studies showing households potentially saving thousands annually by ditching just one car and embracing the transit/walk/bike life (shoutout to the transport policy gurus like Todd Litman!). That's not chump change; that's vacation money, debt reduction, investment potential!

Meet Sarah: From Gridlock Grief to Wallet Win

Picture Sarah, our everyday commuter. She used to wrestle with traffic, her knuckles white on the steering wheel, watching her gas gauge drop and shelling out around $200 a month for the "privilege." Then, she had a lightbulb moment. Her city offered an $80 unlimited monthly pass. Eighty bucks! She took the plunge. Suddenly, her commute involved less stress, maybe even time to read a book or listen to a podcast, and her bank account got an instant $120 boost. Every. Single. Month. That's nearly $1,500 a year back in her pocket, before even thinking about skipped oil changes or avoided parking tickets. Plus, many cities now have slick systems like "fare capping" – tap your card, ride, and the system automatically stops charging you once you hit the price of a pass. Smart tech saving you money without you even trying!

Who's Aboard the Savings Train? Pretty Much Everyone:

This isn't just a trick for one type of person. The Transit Ninja way of life works wonders for:

The City Warrior (aka Urban Professional): Tired of the parking garage hustle and rush hour rage? Imagine gliding past traffic jams, your monthly pass already paid for, saving cash and sanity. Studies actually show lower stress levels for transit commuters compared to drivers stuck in peak-hour chaos. It's like finding a calm oasis in the urban jungle.

The Savvy Student: Ramen budget got you down? Many universities offer super-discounted or even free transit passes (the glorious U-Pass!). This isn't just about saving $50-$100 a month (though that's huge!), it's about freedom to explore, get to class without begging for rides, and avoiding the campus parking nightmare. It's your golden ticket to independence (and maybe more pizza money).

Families Making Every Penny Count: When budgets are tight, transportation can be a crushing weight. Affordable, reliable buses and trains aren't just convenient; they're lifelines. They connect people to better jobs, essential healthcare, education, and even affordable groceries. Good transit is about more than just moving people; it's about moving people forward, boosting opportunity and easing financial strain. It's economic empowerment on wheels.

The Planet Protector: Okay, the green in your wallet is great, but how about keeping the planet greener too?

Choosing the bus or train slashes your carbon footprint compared to driving solo. Every ride is a small act of rebellion against pollution, a vote for cleaner air. You save money and help save the world? That's the ultimate win-win.

The Bottom Line: Your Ride to Riches

Mastering your local transit system isn't just about memorizing routes; it's a powerful financial strategy hiding in plain sight. It's about understanding the real cost of driving versus the smart value of a pass. It's about transforming your commute from a costly chore into a chance to save, relax, and maybe even help the planet.

So, look up your local routes, check out the pass options, and dare to leave the car keys behind sometimes. Becoming a Transit Ninja might just be the smartest (and surprisingly liberating) move you make all year. Your wallet will thank you.

The Two-Wheeled Secret Weapon for Your Everyday Dash

Admit it. You hear the jingle of your car keys almost instinctively when you need milk, have to drop off that package that's been sitting by the door, or meet Sarah for that quick coffee just down the road. It's automatic, right? That short hop in the four-wheeled metal box. But what if those little trips, the ones we barely think about, are actually golden opportunities? What if your bicycle, maybe gathering a little dust, is a secret weapon waiting to make your life simpler, richer, healthier, and surprisingly lighter on the wallet? This isn't just about swapping petrol for pedals; it's about rediscovering a rhythm that benefits you and the world right outside your door.

Hear That? It's Your Wallet Sighing in Relief.

Let's talk cash, because it sings a sweet song here. Forget dry statistics for a second and picture this: every time you don't turn the ignition for that mile-long errand, you're dodging a little cost. It's not just the obvious gulp of fuel; it's the tiny bit of wear on the tires, the fraction of an oil change, the potential parking meter feed. Think of Maria, whipping up lattes three miles from home. By choosing her bike over a car, she's pocketing around $70 a month. Doesn't sound earth-shattering? That's nearly $840 a year – maybe a weekend getaway, a fancy new gadget, or just less financial static. Now zoom out. Consider the behemoth cost of actually owning a car – AAA's 2023 figures suggest the average new car bleeds over $12,000 a year when you count everything. Suddenly, replacing even a few short car trips feels less like a chore and more like finding loose change everywhere you go.

More Than Just Legs: It's Your Body and Brain Singing.

Trading the driver's seat for a saddle on those quick jaunts is like sneaking exercise into your day without noticing. Forget scheduling gym time; your trip to the post office just became a mini-workout. The science backs this up big time: folks who cycle regularly slash their risks of serious stuff like heart disease and certain cancers (hat tip to studies in big journals like The BMJ). You're ticking off those recommended activity minutes without even trying! But it's not just about the body. Remember the feeling of the wind on your face? The sounds of the neighborhood unfiltered by rolled-up windows? That short ride is a mental reset button. It slices through stress, offers a dose of the outdoors, and gives you that little buzz of "I did that!" – it's amazing how much clearer your head can feel after just ten minutes of pedaling.

Breathe Easier, Literally.

Okay, let's face it: cars, especially on short, stop-start trips where the engine never truly warms up, are grumpy polluters. They cough out invisible gunk (the EPA pegs it around 400 grams of CO2 per mile for the average car). Your bicycle? It runs on pure, clean you. Zero fumes. Every single time you choose two wheels over four for that quick errand, you're personally cancelling a little puff of pollution. Imagine your whole street, your whole neighborhood doing the same. The air feels cleaner, the constant traffic drone softens, and suddenly, streets feel more like places for people, not just metal boxes rushing through. Think of cities like Utrecht in the Netherlands – they didn't just build bike lanes; they built a more livable city, one pedal stroke at a time.

It's Not Just Lycra-Clad Warriors: It's Everyone.

This isn't some niche activity. See that student zipping across campus between lectures? Fastest way, guaranteed. Notice more parents using those cool cargo bikes, kids grinning in the front, groceries piled behind? That's a minivan replacement for local life. Look closely in busy city centers – delivery riders on bikes and e-bikes are threading through traffic, proving pedal power is smart logistics. Even workplaces are catching on, offering perks for bike commuters because healthy, less-stressed employees who don't need expensive parking spots are just good business. From the college quad to the courier route, the bicycle is proving it's not a relic; it's a remarkably adaptable tool for modern life.

The Invitation in Your Garage

Choosing your bike for those everyday short trips is more than just practical; it's a quiet revolution. It's a conscious decision that weaves together saving money, boosting your health, clearing your head, and being kinder to the planet. It turns a mundane "gotta go get..." into a moment of movement, awareness, and connection. So, next time your hand reaches for the car keys for that quick hop, pause. Is the bicycle leaning there, waiting? Give it a nod. It might just unlock a richer, healthier, and more vibrant way to navigate your day.

Subtopic 4: Your Car's Secret Weapon: Kitchen Table Tune-Ups & Driveway Hacks

Let's be real: the check engine light isn't the only thing that causes heart palpitations. Sometimes, just the thought of a mechanic's bill is enough to make you sweat. Car ownership feels like a subscription service you can't cancel, right? But what if you could flip the script? What if you held the power to keep your four-wheeled partner humming along happily, dodging those budget-busting repair costs?

Forget thinking of maintenance as a chore. This is your car's personal wellness plan, and you're the guru. It's about small acts of kindness now that prevent catastrophic meltdowns later. Think of it like this: you wouldn't wait for a root canal to start brushing your teeth, right? Same goes for your car. Being proactive isn't just smart; it's your secret weapon for a long-lasting car and a fatter wallet. Let's keep that machine lean, mean, and loving the road.

Now, proving exactly how much you save per screw turn requires a crystal ball, but the big picture? Crystal clear. Folks like the AAA spilled the beans in 2024 – just doing your own oil change can slash that cost by about 25% compared to paying someone else. That's not just skipping a fancy coffee; over time, that's real money staying in your pocket. Picture this: Saturday morning, sunshine, maybe some tunes playing. You spend maybe 30 bucks on oil and a filter. Compare that to the $80+ gut punch at the quick lube joint. Boom. Instant gratification, plus the smug satisfaction of knowing you did that.

But the magic doesn't stop at oil. Let's peek into the DIY mechanic's playbook:

Give Your Engine a Breath Mint (aka Air Filter Swap): Your engine gulps air to make power. If its "lungs" (the air filter) are clogged with gunk, it's like trying to sprint while breathing through a straw. It struggles, wastes fuel, and might feel sluggish. Experts at places like the U.S. Department of Energy confirm: a clean filter lets the engine breathe easy, potentially boosting your gas mileage.

Real Talk: Forget complex studies for a sec. It's basic science – clean air = happy combustion. Groups like the Car Care Council constantly remind us this simple swap can save fuel.

Quick Win Example: Sarah feels her car's lost its pep. Instead of heading to the shop, she grabs a $15 filter online, watches a 2-minute video, and bam! Ten minutes later, dirty filter out, clean one in. She just sidestepped a $50-$70+ bill and her car feels perkier. That's a win-win that keeps adding up.

The Tire Pressure Power Play (Seriously, It's Huge): This is the easiest, most impactful trick in the book. Driving on saggy tires is like running in flip-flops – inefficient, wobbly, and downright dangerous. It tanks your fuel economy and chews up your expensive tires way faster. The government gurus (U.S. Dept. of Energy again) estimate you can boost your MPG by up to 3% just by keeping tires properly aired up. Plus, they wear evenly, meaning that $600+ set lasts way longer.

Real Talk: Underinflated tires are linked to accidents (thanks, NHTSA, for the reminder!) and they literally drag down your fuel efficiency by making the engine work harder.

Quick Win Example: Meet James. Once a month, he takes 5 minutes with a cheap pressure gauge (like, $10) and the free air hose at the gas station. He matches the pressure to the sticker inside his car door. This ridiculously simple, free habit potentially saves him $50+ a year in gas and significantly delays buying new tires. He's basically printing money by pumping air.

Wiper Wisdom: See Clearly, Save Simply: Streaky wipers in a downpour? That's not just annoying, it's a recipe for disaster. Swapping wiper blades is often easier than changing a lightbulb. Lift arm, push tab, slide old off, click new on. Done.

Real Talk: You don't need a PhD to know that seeing where you're going is non-negotiable for safety. Bad wipers are like driving with Vaseline smeared on your windshield.

Quick Win Example: Maria's wipers are doing that awful stutter-and-smear thing. Instead of paying a shop $50 or $60 for the privilege, she grabs a good pair for $30 at the auto parts store and clicks them on herself in the parking lot in under five minutes. Safer driving and cash saved? Yes, please.

See the pattern? These aren't complex engine rebuilds. This is basic car care – the stuff that stops small annoyances from snowballing into big, expensive headaches. By catching things like dirty filters or low tire pressure early, you're being kind to your engine, your suspension, your fuel budget, and your peace of mind. You're preventing breakdowns, making every drop of fuel count, and ultimately, keeping your trusty ride rolling reliably for years longer.

That's how you keep your car lean – running efficiently, costing less, and putting you confidently in the driver's seat of its well-being.

Healthcare Hustle—Affordable Wellness in 2025

Beyond the Maze: Your Health Savings Account as a Financial Game-Changer

Let's be honest, navigating healthcare costs can feel like trying to solve a Rubik's cube blindfolded. It's confusing, often stressful, and leaves you wondering if you're making the right moves for your health and your wallet. But what if there was a hidden pathway, a financial tool tucked away that could actually turn healthcare planning into a source of strength, not stress?

Meet the Health Savings Account (HSA), especially when it teams up with its partner, the high-deductible health plan (HDHP). Think of the HDHP like the key to a secret garden: yes, you might have a higher gate (deductible) to step over before the main insurance benefits fully bloom, but that key unlocks access to the HSA – and that's where the real magic happens. This isn't just about stashing cash for copays; it's a savvy financial strategy, a way to actively build wellness and wealth.

The Secret Sauce: Why HSAs Feel Like a Financial Superpower

The buzz around HSAs often centers on their "triple tax advantage," and for good reason. It's like finding a financial cheat code, officially blessed by the IRS (check out Publication 969 if you love the details!):

Pay Less Tax Now: Every dollar you put into your HSA (either pre-tax from your paycheck or deducted later if you contribute directly) magically shrinks your taxable income for the year. Imagine getting an instant reward just for planning for future health needs! It's like the government giving you a high-five (in the form of tax savings) for being proactive.

Watch it Grow, Tax-Free: This is where it gets exciting. Money sitting in your HSA doesn't just sit there (unless you want it to). Many HSAs let you invest your funds. Picture a greenhouse where your savings can blossom – stocks, bonds, mutual funds – completely shielded from the yearly tax sun. Any growth, interest, or dividends stay yours, untouched by taxes, letting your money work harder for you over time. Investment pros often show how this tax-free growth can seriously outperform identical investments in regular accounts over the long haul.
Spend it Tax-Free (on Health Stuff): When you need to pay for qualified medical expenses – think doctor visits, prescriptions, dental work, eye exams, even things like acupuncture or long-term care premiums down the road – you can pull money out of your HSA completely tax-free. No income tax, nada. It's money you saved tax-free, grew tax-free, and now spend tax-free on keeping yourself healthy.

While nailing down a precise "30% savings" figure for everyone is tricky (your personal savings depend on your tax bracket, state rules, etc.), the power is undeniable. Financial wizards often estimate the combined tax shield (federal, maybe state, FICA) can easily save you 20%, 30%, even 40%+ on every dollar you contribute. For 2025, you can stash away up to $4,300 if you have self-only HDHP coverage, or a hefty $8,550 for family coverage (plus an extra $1,000 if you're 55+ – a little boost!). People are catching on; research groups like EBRI keep showing more folks opening HSAs and growing bigger balances, often investing a good chunk – proving these accounts are becoming serious long-term financial allies.

Bringing the HSA Strategy to Life: Meet the Trailblazers

This isn't just theory; it's about real people making smart choices:

Maya, The Security Seeker: Working part-time as a cashier, Maya chooses an HDHP for its lower monthly premium, easing her budget. She sets up a $100 monthly transfer to her HSA. It might sound small, but that's $1,200 a year building before taxes touch it. This isn't just savings; it's her peace-of-mind fund. A sudden cavity? A surprise prescription? Maya has a dedicated, tax-advantaged cushion, potentially saving her hundreds in taxes each year just by building that safety net.

Ben, The Future Builder: Ben, a graphic designer in his late 20s, is healthy now and sees his HDHP/HSA combo as a launchpad. He contributes close to the max. He uses a tiny bit for his yearly dental check-up and snazzy new glasses, but the rest? He invests it, aiming for long-term growth. He knows the power of compounding, especially in a tax-free environment. He pictures this account not just covering future aches and pains, but potentially becoming a significant resource for healthcare in retirement, tax-free. (Bonus: after age 65, he could even use it for non-medical things, just paying regular income tax like a 401k).

The Chens, The Family Coordinators: With two active kids, the Chen family treats their HSA like their family's healthcare command center. They anticipate costs – check-ups, maybe braces down the line, the occasional urgent care dash – and contribute enough to cover these tax-free. They also aim to invest any surplus. Unlike FSAs that often have a "use-it-or-lose-it" deadline, their HSA funds roll over year after year, offering incredible flexibility for the unpredictable rhythm of family health needs.

The Takeaway: It's Your Move

Choosing an HDHP isn't just about accepting a higher deductible. It's about unlocking the door to the HSA – a powerful tool waiting to be wielded. It's your chance to cut your taxes, manage healthcare costs intelligently, build an emergency reserve, and cultivate a tax-free investment portfolio all in one go. It's about transforming a potential financial headache into a strategic advantage, giving you more control, more security, and a clearer path to financial wellness. Why just navigate the healthcare maze when you can master it?

Your Wallet's Secret Weapon: Finding Prescription Gold Hiding in Plain Sight

Let's be honest, that moment at the pharmacy counter can feel like bracing for impact. You hand over the script, hold your breath, and hope the number that comes back doesn't send your budget into a tailspin. It's a healthcare headache we know all too well. But what if I told you there's a key to unlocking significant savings, a kind of 'treasure map' already approved by the experts, waiting right there behind the counter? Forget risky shortcuts; we're talking about the smart, savvy world of generic medications – your personal goldmine for affordable wellness.

"Generic"? Isn't That Just... Lesser?

Hold that thought! Think about your favorite frosted flakes cereal. You know the one in the bright, flashy box with the cartoon mascot? Now picture the store's own brand right next to it. Different packaging, maybe a less famous tiger, but inside? The exact same crunchy, sugary flakes that make your morning sing. That's the heart of generic drugs.

For a medication to earn the "generic" label from tough regulators like the FDA, it's not just similar to the brand name – it has to be its molecular twin. It uses the identical active ingredient, the core component that actually does the healing work. They must prove they work the same way in your body, absorbed at the same rate, reaching the same levels in your bloodstream (that's the science-speak "bioequivalence" part). Imagine it's the exact same recipe, baked in a different kitchen, but passing the same rigorous taste and quality tests. Sure, the 'frosting' might be a slightly different color (inactive ingredients like dyes or fillers can vary), but unless you have a specific allergy, it's the same powerful medicine doing the job.

Okay, But Why the Dramatic Price Drop? It Feels Too Good To Be True...

Here's the secret: It's all about who paid for the adventure map. The brand-name companies spent fortunes on the initial discovery, the years of research, the clinical trials, and the massive marketing campaigns to introduce their drug. They get a period of exclusivity (a patent) to recoup those big bucks.

Generic makers? They get to use the map after the trail has been blazed. They don't have those colossal upfront discovery costs. They follow the established recipe, prove their version is identical in action, and pass the same safety and quality checks. The result? They can offer you the same medicinal benefit for, typically, a staggering 80-85% less. That FDA mention of 80% savings? That's the real deal, repeated day in and day out.

This isn't just pocket change. We're talking about the kind of savings that could mean less stress about bills, maybe affording that extra grocery bag, or simply breathing easier financially. Collectively, choosing generics has saved the U.S. healthcare system trillions – yes, with a 'T' – over the last decade. That's powerful.

Bringing the Gold Home: Real People, Real Savings

Remember that retiree saving $50 a month on blood pressure meds? That's not just a statistic; that's $600 a year back in their pocket. That could be holiday gifts for grandkids, necessary home repairs, or simply the peace of mind that comes with a little extra cushion. It's about making healthcare accessible. When medicine is affordable, people can actually take it consistently, leading to better health outcomes. Think about it:

Keeping Hearts Healthy: Switching from a pricey brand-name cholesterol drug to its generic counterpart means the same heart protection, often for hundreds less per year. That same logic applies to managing diabetes, thyroid issues, or breathing easier with asthma.

Quieting Minds: Accessing generic antidepressants or anti-anxiety meds makes vital long-term mental healthcare sustainable, removing a huge financial barrier to feeling better.

Getting Back on Your Feet: Even for a short course of antibiotics after an infection or pain relief after surgery, choosing generic means healing up without your wallet feeling quite so bruised.

Claim Your Treasure

The "Generic Goldmine" isn't hype; it's a smart, science-backed reality. These aren't "lesser" drugs; they are the same effective treatments, rigorously tested and approved, offered at a fair price.

So, next time you're getting a prescription, feel empowered! Ask your doctor or pharmacist, "Is there a generic version available for this?" It's not about cutting corners; it's about being an informed, savvy healthcare consumer. It's your health, your budget, and often, there's gold waiting right there for you to claim. Go ahead, unlock those savings!

Healthcare Doesn't Have to Empty Your Pockets: How Seeing Your Doc Online is Like Finding Cash in Your Coat

Let's be honest, getting sick is stressful enough without the looming dread of the bill. That trip to the doctor's office? It's not just the co-pay. It's the gas money, maybe parking fees, potentially taking unpaid time off work, and that nagging feeling you might catch something else in the waiting room. It all adds up, turning healthcare into a financial hurdle.

But what if there was a way to skip the waiting room shuffle and the travel hassle, getting care right from your couch, and saving a decent chunk of change? That's the magic of virtual care, or telehealth. Think of it as the ultimate healthcare shortcut – a digital house call that's kinder to your schedule and your bank account.

It's not just wishful thinking; the numbers back it up. Big names like the American Medical Association have crunched the data, finding that a virtual visit can leave you about $70 richer compared to dragging yourself into an office. Why? Because logging into an app is way cheaper than keeping a whole clinic running. Less overhead for the docs can mean less cost passed on to you.

Picture this: Your little one wakes up with a weird rash. The old way? Panic, bundle everyone up, drive across town, wait nervously, see the doctor for maybe 10 minutes, drive back, and then face a bill that makes you wince – easily $100 or more gone.

Now, the telehealth way: You grab your phone or laptop while still in your PJs. You connect with a clinician, show them the rash via video, get reassurance and maybe an e-prescription sent straight to your pharmacy. You might pay a flat fee, say around $30. Boom. You just saved yourself time, stress, exposure to other germs, and kept that $70 (or more!) right where it belongs – with you. That's gas money, part of the grocery bill, or maybe just a little breathing room. Studies confirm it – people save real money on travel and lost wages when they go virtual.

And it's not just for sniffles and bumps. Got a chronic condition like high blood pressure or diabetes? Those regular check-ins can feel like a relentless cycle of travel, time off, and clinic fees. Telehealth flips the script. Imagine sending your blood pressure readings from a home device and having a quick video chat with your doctor. Fewer costly trips, same effective care. It's even shown to help folks with conditions like heart failure stay out of the hospital, dodging those massive readmission bills.

Mental health gets a huge boost too. Therapy is most effective when it's consistent, but getting to appointments can be tough – the travel, the time, maybe feeling awkward walking into a clinic. Teletherapy rips down those barriers. Getting support from the privacy and comfort of your own home, often at a lower cost, makes sticking with it so much easier. Better long-term mental wellness can mean avoiding more expensive crisis care later. It's a win-win, especially for people far from city centers or those who find clinics hard to reach.

Speaking of distance, if you live out in the country, telehealth isn't just convenient; it's a game-changer.

Seeing a specialist might normally mean hours on the road, maybe even an overnight stay. The cost? Astronomical, before you even pay the doctor. A virtual consult wipes out those huge travel expenses, bringing expert care right to your screen, no matter your zip code.

Even healing from surgery gets easier. Instead of struggling back to the hospital for a quick post-op wound check, imagine a secure video call where the doc takes a look and chats with you. Less pain, less hassle, less cost, all while you recover comfortably at home.

So, what's the bottom line? Telehealth uses technology to cut out the expensive extras tied to traditional healthcare. By swapping physical visits for virtual ones when it makes sense, it saves you cold, hard cash directly (lower fees) and indirectly (no travel, no time off). It's not just a futuristic idea; it's happening now, making healthcare feel a little less like a heavy backpack and a lot more like accessible, affordable support when you need it most.

Your Body Isn't Just a Temple, It's Your Best Investment Account

Let's be honest, the shadow of healthcare costs looms large. We see the headlines, maybe feel the pinch ourselves – prescriptions that cost a small fortune, unexpected trips to the emergency room, the bewildering maze of insurance bills. We're often caught in a reactive loop, scrambling to fix things after they break. But what if we flipped the script? What if we started thinking about our health less like an unpredictable expense and more like a high-yield savings account we actively contribute to?

This isn't some airy-fairy wellness trend; it's "Wellness First," a deeply practical, financially savvy way of living. It's the radical idea that taking care of ourselves now—really investing in our physical and mental well-being—is the smartest way to dodge crippling medical bills later. It's about building health equity, one good choice at a time.

Think about the simple magic of movement. Forget dry statistics for a moment (though the research, like findings often shared by the CDC or in journals like the Journal of the American Heart Association, consistently backs this up). Imagine that daily walk you take isn't just "exercise." It's you, actively lowering your future risk of heart trouble that could cost thousands. It's strengthening your defenses against the slow creep of diabetes, potentially saving you decades of medication costs and specialist visits. Each step is like depositing a coin in your "future health fund," reducing the likelihood of costly withdrawals down the road. It's not just about avoiding the big, scary diagnoses; it's about fewer sick days, less reliance on quick fixes, and more energy to actually live.

And it goes way beyond just breaking a sweat.

Kicking the Habit, Keeping the Cash: Choosing to quit smoking isn't just adding years to your life; it's directly subtracting future dollars spent managing lung disease or cancer (billions are spent nationally, according to CDC figures, imagine the personal cost!). It's freedom, both for your lungs and your bank account.

Eating Colorfully, Saving Green: Filling your plate with vibrant fruits and veggies, the good stuff nature intended (as health bodies like the WHO champion), isn't just delicious. It's building a shield against obesity, heart disease, and diabetes – conditions notorious for their long-term, wallet-draining management. Think of it as delicious, edible insurance.

An Ounce of Prevention, a Ton of Saved Trouble: Remember vaccinations? Those quick shots are tiny investments that prevent potentially massive payouts for treating illnesses like the flu, measles, or even certain cancers (research highlighted by institutions like the NIH confirms their cost-effectiveness). It's simple math: a small upfront effort saves a potential mountain of cost and suffering.

This "invest now, save later" principle plays out everywhere:

In Your Own Life: That person taking mindful moments to de-stress? They might be sidestepping stress-induced ailments and the doctor visits that follow. That simple daily walk we talked about? Cumulatively, over years, it can translate into thousands saved by delaying or preventing chronic conditions, far outweighing the "cost" of a pair of walking shoes. You're not just managing health; you're managing future expenses.

Where You Work: Ever wonder why companies offer wellness programs? It's not just goodwill. Smart businesses know (and studies by groups like the RAND Corporation often show) that healthier employees mean lower insurance claims, fewer sick days, and better productivity. Investing a little in gym discounts or health screenings upfront often saves them a lot more down the line. Healthy people power healthy profits.

In Your Community: Think bigger! Parks and safe walking paths aren't just nice amenities; they're public health investments. Farmers' markets bringing fresh food to neighborhoods aren't just quaint; they're fighting future healthcare burdens. Community-wide health initiatives are like collective savings plans, aiming to reduce the future strain on hospitals and public funds by tackling problems like obesity or preventable diseases at their roots.

So, let's reframe how we see taking care of ourselves. That trip to the gym, choosing the salad, scheduling that check-up, managing stress – these aren't expenses or chores. They are deposits. They are wise investments in the most valuable asset you possess: your own life, brimming with potential and free from the unnecessary weight of avoidable future costs.

Investing in your wellness first isn't just about feeling good today; it's about building a richer, healthier, and more financially secure tomorrow. It turns out, the path to well-being might just be the smartest financial plan you ever make.

The Inflation Buffer—Emergency Funds That Last

Finding Your Footing: That First $1,000 is More Than Money, It's Breathing Room

Life's got a wicked sense of humor, right? One minute you're sailing smoothly, the next – BAM! – a flat tire grinds your morning commute to a halt. Or maybe the fridge suddenly decides its chilling days are over. Or worse, an unexpected doctor's bill lands like a lead weight in your mailbox. We've all been there. Without a little bit of financial wiggle room, these everyday hiccups can feel like full-blown earthquakes, sending shockwaves of stress, maybe even nudging us towards credit cards with terrifying interest rates or forcing choices we really don't want to make.

This is where the magic of your first $1,000 comes in. Forget, for a second, those giant emergency fund goals that feel like climbing Mount Everest in flip-flops. Let's talk about building your initial "Okay, I Can Handle This" Fund. Think of it as your personal financial first-aid kit. It's not about building an impenetrable castle overnight; it's about forging that crucial first layer of defense – a goal that feels reachable, something you can actually wrap your head and hands around, offering immediate relief and a massive dose of "I got this" energy.

Why $1,000? Because it breaks the spell of overwhelm. Staring down the barrel of saving 3-6 months of living expenses can feel so huge, so impossible, that we just... don't start. This smaller, $1,000 milestone transforms that vague, terrifying mountain into a manageable hill we can actually climb. It's a concrete target for the here and now. And nailing it? That's pure gold. It does something powerful psychologically – it proves to you that saving is possible. It builds momentum, like the first snowball rolling downhill, gathering speed and size. It taps into that fundamental human drive where small wins fuel bigger ambitions (yeah, there's science behind it, like Goal Setting Theory – basically, hitting small targets makes us hungry for more!). That feeling of accomplishment? It's rocket fuel.

And this isn't just feel-good theory; the need is real. Forget dry statistics for a moment and picture this: reports (like the ones the Federal Reserve puts out) consistently show that a chunk of adults would be thrown into a tailspin by a surprise $400 expense. Four hundred bucks! That's less than a set of new tires, maybe one urgent care visit, or a minor home repair. If that small amount can derail a budget, it highlights just how many folks are walking a financial tightrope without a net. Your $1,000 "Okay, I Can Handle This" fund gives you a much sturdier platform, a buffer against those slightly larger (but still annoyingly common) curveballs. Researchers have confirmed time and again: having actual liquid cash saved is the most effective shock absorber when life gets bumpy.

So, how do people actually build this thing in the real world?

Meet Maria, the Server: Juggling tables and tips, she remembers vividly when a $500 car repair forced her to borrow cash. Never again, she decided. Now, she treats her savings like another bill. Every week, rain or shine, $30 from her earnings gets tucked away – maybe cash in an envelope, maybe a quick transfer via her banking app into an account nicknamed "Freedom Fund." In about eight months, diligently setting aside that weekly amount (roughly $130/month), she hit her $1,000 goal. The peace of mind, she says, tastes better than any fancy dessert she serves.

Meet Alex, the Freelance Writer: Income for Alex is a rollercoaster – feast one month, famine the next. Inspired by business tactics, Alex applies a "pay yourself first" rule, personally. Every single time a client payment hits the bank, 8% is immediately whisked away into the $1,000 fund before anything else gets paid. Using automatic bank rules makes it painless. It took about six months, and now, during slower work periods, that buffer means Alex isn't forced to take low-paying projects just to keep the lights on. It's financial dignity.

Meet Chloe, the Recent Grad: New job, student loans, rent... Chloe felt the squeeze. But she got tactical. Packing lunch instead of buying ($40-$50 saved/week), ditching one streaming service she rarely watched ($15/month), and setting up an automatic $25 transfer every payday. She treated it like a game – finding small savings here and there. That daily $5 coffee? Redirected. In less than five months, she crossed the $1,000 finish line. The feeling? Pure empowerment, proving she could take control even on an entry-level salary.

That first $1,000 isn't the final chapter in your financial story. But it might just be the most important first page you write. It's the concrete proof that you can build stability, the deep breath you take when life throws a minor punch, and the solid ground you need to stand on before reaching for even bigger savings goals down the road. It's your starting block, your confidence booster, your tangible piece of "Okay, World. Bring it on."

Subtopic 2: Give Your Savings a Serious Pep Talk (Hello, Yield Boosters!)

Does your savings account feel... well, sleepy? Like that cash you've worked so hard to squirrel away is just lounging on a comfy couch, barely lifting a finger? In many old-school savings accounts, that's pretty much the reality. They might offer a tiny whisper of interest, the kind that gets drowned out by the everyday rise in prices (hello, inflation!). It's like trying to fill a bucket with a leaky eyedropper.

But what if you could give that money an energy drink? That's where "Yield Boosters" stride onto the scene. Think of them as personal trainers for your cash reserves, designed to get those numbers pumping without necessarily throwing them into the wild rollercoaster of the stock market. And the undisputed champion in this training camp? The High-Yield Savings Account (HYSA).

So, what's the magic? It's right there in the name: High Yield. Forget the microscopic crumbs of interest you might get from that giant bank on the corner with the marble floors. HYSAs, especially those offered by nimble online banks or community-focused credit unions, play a different game. They compete for your savings by offering significantly juicier growth rates – what the finance folks call Annual Percentage Yield (APY).

How can they afford to be so generous? Imagine a bank without all the expensive downtown real estate and huge branch networks. Online banks run lean. They don't have those massive overhead costs, so they can pass those savings directly to you in the form of better interest rates. It's simple math, really – less spent on buildings means more can be shared with savers. (Trust us, the number crunchers at places like Bankrate and NerdWallet have confirmed this time and again).

Fast forward to today, and the trend continues. Even the bigwigs like the Federal Deposit Insurance Corporation (FDIC) noticed back in 2024 how competition was pushing these rates upward. They saw signs pointing towards potential yields hitting around 4.8% APY in 2025 for some savings options. Now, the FDIC doesn't set these rates – think of them more as the referee and the insurance provider. They watch the game, and crucially, they provide that safety net: insuring your deposits in their member banks up to $250,000 per person, per bank, per account type. This insurance is like a security blanket for your money, making HYSAs a fantastic spot for cash you absolutely need to keep safe, even if the bank's name isn't one you see on every street corner. (That FDIC sticker? It's a major reason people feel confident putting their money there, according to consumer finance watchdogs).

Let's make that 4.8% feel real. Remember our diligent clerk who saved $1,000?

In a sleepy, traditional account earning a hypothetical 0.1% APY (which is sadly realistic sometimes), after a whole year, they'd have earned... wait for it... $1. Enough for a gumball, maybe.

But! Park that same $1,000 in an HYSA humming along at 4.8% APY, and boom! After a year, they've got an extra $48. That's not just loose change; that's a nice dinner out, a couple of movie tickets, or a decent chunk towards another goal – earned simply by choosing a smarter parking spot for their cash. This isn't some complicated financial alchemy; it's just making your safe money pull its own weight.

Where Does This Shine in Real Life?

The Emergency Fund Power-Up: Picture Sarah, building her $6,000 "life happens" fund. She's saving $500 each month. Putting that growing stash into an HYSA at 4.8% means it's not just her contributions building the pile. The interest earned joins the party, like a helpful little sidekick, pushing her towards her goal faster. And once she hits $6k? The fund itself keeps generating a little extra cash, all on its own. Seeing that growth, even if small at first, is like a high-five for your brain, making you want to keep saving.

The Down Payment Accelerator: Mark and Lisa are dreaming of their first home, saving up $20,000 for the down payment over the next two years. The stock market feels way too unpredictable for money they need soon. An HYSA is their sweet spot. Their hard-saved principal is shielded by that FDIC blanket, and the 4.8% yield gives their savings a serious boost. Over two years, assuming the rate stays put and compounding works its magic, they could earn nearly $2,000 in interest! That's a significant chunk of closing costs or moving expenses covered, just by letting their savings work smarter in a safe place. Financial planners practically shout this from the rooftops for short-term goals: safety first, then optimized growth.

The Freelancer's Tax Trick: Meet Alex, a graphic designer navigating the gig economy. Alex knows about setting aside money (say, 30%) from each project for taxes. Instead of letting that tax stash nap in a checking account doing absolutely nothing, Alex sweeps it into an HYSA. It's still earmarked for Uncle Sam, but until tax day rolls around, it's quietly earning interest. If Alex sets aside $15,000 over the year, that 4.8% APY could mean an extra $720 by the time taxes are due. Think of it as turning a chore (saving for taxes) into a mini-opportunity.

The Bottom Line:

Using a high-yield savings account is like finding the turbo button for your safe money. Sure, interest rates can wiggle up and down based on what the big central banks are doing and how banks are competing. But the core idea – earning way more on your readily available cash than you would in a traditional account – is a game-changer. The numbers (like that potential 4.8%) and the real-life stories show the clear advantage. It's about making your savings hustle for you, transforming them from lazy loungers into active earners. It's one of the simplest, yet most powerful, steps you can take to reach your financial goals quicker, with minimal risk. Why let your money sleep when it could be working?

From Dust Bunnies to Dough: Unlocking the Cash Hidden in Your Clutter

Take a slow walk through your home. No, really. Look past the familiar and see it with fresh eyes. That exercise bike doubling as a clothes rack? The box of cables from gadgets long gone? The bridesmaid dress you swore you'd wear again (you won't)? It feels like... stuff. Maybe even stressful stuff. But what if I told you that "stuff" isn't just taking up space – it's holding your money hostage?

Forget Wall Street wizards flipping mansions. We're talking about a different kind of "asset flip," one that happens right under your own roof. It's the magic trick of turning things you don't use into cash you can use. Think of it as reclaiming lost dollars, rescuing forgotten value from the land of dust bunnies. This isn't about launching a global empire from your garage (unless you want to!); it's about giving your savings account a little boost, knocking down debt faster, funding that weekend getaway, or just enjoying the sweet satisfaction of making money from thin air (or, you know, from that juicer you used twice).

And here's the kicker: clearing out that clutter doesn't just line your pockets; it clears your head. Seriously! Scientists have actually linked messy environments to higher stress levels (yep, that frazzled feeling is real). Imagine your brain trying to focus with a dozen half-finished projects visually shouting for attention. Princeton researchers found that physical clutter literally fights for your focus, making you feel drained and stressed. So, when you declutter and sell, you're not just making space in your home; you're carving out breathing room in your mind. Getting paid for that? That's just chef's kiss. Plus, taking control, turning unwanted items into actual cash – it feels good. It's a small win that fuels bigger financial confidence.

Don't shrug this off as just finding spare change. While that $280 average someone found on eBay is a nice starting point (though, always ask: per sale? per month?), the bigger picture is massive. The whole world is falling back in love with second-hand. Think about it: sustainable shopping is cool now. People, especially younger generations, are actively choosing pre-loved items, from designer jeans on ThredUp to refurbished smartphones, to reduce waste and save cash. You're not just selling old stuff; you're participating in a huge, growing movement – a circular economy where things get a second life.

How does this look in real life? Let's paint a picture:

The Nest Egg Builder: Remember Sarah, whose baby is now a toddler? That barely-used high chair, the outgrown snowsuit, the swing set taking over the garden? She snaps a few photos, posts them on a local parent's group, and boom – $50 here, $20 there. It goes straight into a "Future Fun Fund" for the kids. She's turning yesterday's necessities into tomorrow's opportunities, one sale at a time.

The Savvy Student: Finals are over. Instead of selling textbooks back to the campus store for pennies, Alex lists them online. Adds in that old gaming console and the mini-fridge from freshman year. Suddenly, there's a few hundred extra bucks to ease the sting of tuition or just afford pizza beyond the first week of the month. That's clutter converted directly into breathing room.

The Dream Chaser: Maya dreams of getting a great camera. Budget's tight. But wait – there's that keyboard gathering dust, the vintage board games never played, the fancy art supplies from a forgotten hobby. She lists them on places like eBay or specialized sites. Each sale is a step closer. Old passions are literally funding a new one, without touching her paycheck.

So, look around. That clutter isn't just clutter. It's potential energy. It's untapped resources. It's a practical, powerful way to grab hold of your finances and maybe even find a little peace of mind in the process. Systematically finding, prepping, and selling what you no longer need isn't just tidying up – it's transforming dormant stuff into dynamic cash to power up your goals. Ready to flip your clutter?

Does money sometimes feel like this impossible mountain to climb? Like getting ahead means giving up everything fun? Yeah, been there. But what if building a safety net, that little cushion that lets you breathe easier, wasn't about a total life overhaul?

Enter the "Single Snip" idea. Forget dramatic budget slashing. This is about finding one thing – just one – that you regularly spend money on but could live without, and making a conscious switch. Think of it like finding a hidden treasure chest in your weekly routine.

We all have them, right? That fancy coffee that's more ritual than necessity, the lunch orders that pile up faster than emails, the subscription box you forget is coming, the automatic "yes" to another round of drinks. They seem tiny on their own. A few bucks here, a tenner there. Our brains are funny; they like to file these under "small stuff, doesn't count" (fancy folks call this "mental accounting"). But spoiler alert: it all counts. That drip, drip, drip of small spends? It can fill a bucket faster than you think. Ever actually added up how much that daily treat really costs you over a year? The numbers can be genuinely shocking (some studies show people dropping over a grand a year just on coffee!).

This "Single Snip" trick is about catching one of those drips. Pick one consistent spend that isn't truly essential. Maybe it's those $15 Friday cocktails. Sounds small, right? But snip that one habit, and suddenly you've rerouted $780 a year.

Now, what does $780 feel like?

It feels like peace of mind: Imagine that money sitting there when your car suddenly makes that noise, or a surprise bill lands on your doormat. That $780 is the difference between panic and "Okay, I can handle this." It's the start of your emergency fund, your financial superhero cape.

It feels like freedom: Got that nagging credit card debt breathing down your neck? Throwing that $780 directly at the monster shrinks it faster, saving you a chunk in interest and getting you closer to that amazing feeling of being debt-free. It's a powerful punch against high-interest chains.

It feels like hope: Okay, $780 might not sound like a fortune to invest. But tucking it away consistently in something simple like a low-cost fund is like planting a tiny seed. With time and the magic of compounding (where your money starts making money), that small, consistent act can grow into something surprisingly substantial down the road. It's building your future self a little security, one saved drink at a time.

See? No need to turn your life upside down or live like a monk. The power is in the focus. By making one intentional change, snipping one non-essential habit, you prove to yourself you can take control. You turn mindless spending into mindful saving. It's less about the sacrifice and more about the surprising, empowering gain you get from one small, consistent act of financial self-care. It's your money, your choice – find your snip and watch what grows.

Collective Resilience—Community as Your Ally

Think about that feeling – you need something, maybe desperately want it, but the thought of cracking open your wallet makes you wince. Or maybe you're sitting on something valuable – a skill you've mastered, extra produce from your garden, a room you're not using – and wish you could just poof it into what you actually need.

That, right there, is the ancient, beating heart of barter. It's the original commerce, the first "deal," born long before coins jingled or plastic swiped. And guess what? It's not some dusty relic. It's back, humming with new energy, fueled by tight budgets, a craving for real connection, and the digital webs that link us all. It's less about penny-pinching (though it definitely helps!) and more about a smart, resourceful dance: trading what you have directly for what you need.

Turning 'Nothing' into 'Something Wonderful'

Let's be real, the money side of things is pretty darn attractive. Forget dusty reports for a moment – think about value. That pile of stuff you haven't sold? That afternoon slot you can't fill? That's not just clutter or wasted time; it's potential energy, waiting. The folks who run organized trade networks (like the members of the International Reciprocal Trade Association) see this all the time. Businesses are swapping unsold hotel rooms for advertising space, extra inventory for essential office supplies. They're essentially pulling value out of thin air, saving anywhere from 15% to over 30% in cold, hard cash they didn't have to spend. It's like financial alchemy – turning potential loss into real gain. And when times get tough and cash flow slows to a trickle? Barter keeps the wheels turning, a vital pulse in the economy.

The Everyday Magic: Bread for Brainpower

Imagine Sarah, a baker whose sourdough is legendary but whose teenager is bombing algebra. Every evening, a few gorgeous loaves go unsold. Down the street lives Tom, a math tutor whose family devours fresh bread. Instead of Sarah shelling out $120 cash for tutoring, and Tom buying bread, they strike a simple, beautiful deal. Sarah sends over a steady supply of crusty goodness, and Tom tackles quadratic equations with her son. Poof! Needs met. Value exchanged. No cash register involved. Sarah kept her $120, Tom got his daily bread using his skill. It's the perfect "you scratch my back, I'll scratch yours," writ small and delicious.

Beyond the Bakery: Barter Goes Big (and Small)

This isn't just about neighbourhood favours. Barter scales beautifully:

Main Street Mojo: Think of Alex, the graphic designer whose office walls are screaming for a makeover. Then there's Maria, the painter whose business needs a killer website like yesterday. They connect, maybe through a local business group. Alex designs Maria's sleek new online look (worth, say, $2,500). Maria transforms Alex's drab office into an inspiring workspace (a job worth the same). Both get exactly what they need, boosting their businesses without draining their bank accounts. Money stays put, ready for payroll or that new piece of equipment. It's a B2B power move.

Corporate Chess Game: Picture a big hotel chain with empty rooms haunting the off-season. Now picture a media giant with unsold ad time. Enter the corporate barter wizards. They orchestrate a grand exchange. The hotel offers up room nights, getting "trade credits" – like specialized IOUs. The media company offers ad space, getting credits too. Now, the hotel can use its credits to launch a massive ad campaign it might not have afforded otherwise. The media company uses its credits to house executives traveling for business or reward top employees. It's a sophisticated way to turn empty seats and silent airwaves (ghosts of lost income) into tangible assets.

Community Currency: The Power of an Hour: Dive into a local "Time Bank." Here, the currency isn't dollars, it's time. You spend an hour helping Mrs. Gable with her garden? You earn one Time Credit. You can then "spend" that credit getting an hour of help from someone else – maybe fixing your leaky faucet, getting tech support, or finding a babysitter. It's profoundly simple and deeply human. Studies show these networks weave communities tighter, combat loneliness, and offer a safety net, proving that everyone's time, and everyone's contribution, truly has value.

So, the "Barter Boom"? It's not just a catchy phrase. It's a living, breathing testament to human ingenuity and resilience. It's ancient wisdom remixed for the modern age, proving that sometimes the smartest way to get what you need is simply to connect and trade, human to human, skill to skill, need to need – leaving the bank out of it altogether.

Beyond the Dusty Shelf: Why Sharing Stuff is Our Secret Superpower

Peer into the shadowy corners of your home – the garage rafters, the back of the closet, that shed out back. What forgotten treasures reside there? The pressure washer that roared to life precisely once last summer? The towering ladder bought for a single, nerve-wracking bulb change? That ridiculously fancy cake stand dreaming of its next (and possibly only) starring role? We all do it: collect these "just-in-case" soldiers, paying the full price of admission, upkeep, and precious space, only to let them gather dust in lonely silence.

But what if there's a smarter, friendlier, more human way? Enter the beautifully simple magic of resource pooling. Forget dry economics for a second; think of it as a neighbourhood treasure chest. It's the radical idea that maybe, just maybe, we don't all need our own everything. It's neighbours, friends, or even local businesses looking at each other and saying, "Hey, instead of ten of us buying that expensive widget we only use twice a year, let's get one really good one together." It's shifting from "mine" to "ours," unlocking a shared wealth we didn't know we had.

Your Wallet Will Breathe Easier

Let's be real: the money argument hits home. Why should every house on the block have its own lawnmower, singing its solo tune for maybe an hour a week? Imagine splitting the cost of one top-notch mower with a few neighbours. Suddenly, that $250 machine costs you a fraction, leaving more cash for, well, living. It's not just wishful thinking. Studies and real-world sharing hubs consistently show folks saving serious coin (think 30-40% or more!) on things like tools when they borrow instead of buy. And it's not just the sticker price. Think of the vanished costs of repairs you won't have to make, the storage space reclaimed, the mental energy saved. It's like finding money you didn't know you'd lost.

More Than Money: Greener Living & Real Connections

The ripple effect goes way beyond our bank accounts. Every shared tool is potentially one less item manufactured – meaning fewer raw materials ripped from the earth, less energy burned, and less junk eventually clogging landfills. Think of car-sharing: studies show one shared car can kick 9 to 13 privately owned ones off the road! That's cleaner air, less traffic stress, and cities that feel more like places for people, not just parking lots.

But perhaps the most beautiful part? Sharing rebuilds something precious: community. Organizing a tool library or even just agreeing to share a ladder with Bob next door requires talking, trusting, cooperating. It turns streets from collections of separate houses into genuine neighbourhoods where people know each other's names, lend a hand (or a hammer), and build real social fabric. It's the alchemy of turning shared stuff into shared stories and support.

Where the Magic Happens: Pooling in Action

This isn't some futuristic dream; it's happening right now, in countless creative ways:

Tool Libraries (The Arsenal of Awesome): Imagine a library, but instead of books, it's packed with everything from basic screwdrivers to beastly demolition hammers. Pay a small yearly fee, and BAM! You have access to thousands of tools without cluttering your home or emptying your wallet. These places are humming hubs of empowerment.

Car Sharing (Wheels When You Need Them): Services like Zipcar or local community car clubs free you from the heavy chains of car ownership (payments, insurance, parking!). Grab a car for an hour or a day, hassle-free. It's about access, not excess.

Libraries of Things (Beyond the Toolbox): Why stop at tools? These amazing places lend out sewing machines, camping gear, stand mixers, projectors, giant Jenga sets – you name it! They're playgrounds for trying new hobbies and living large without buying large.

The OG Sharing: Your Street! That first lawnmower example? It's happening everywhere, quietly. Neighbours coordinating on snow blowers, trading gardening tools over the fence, sharing bulk buys. This is the grassroots, trust-based sharing that knits communities together, one borrowed item at a time.

Ultimately, resource pooling isn't just a clever hack to save money. It's a mindset shift. It's choosing access over accumulation, community over consumption, and sustainability over stuffocation. It's about tapping into our collective power to live lighter on the planet, easier on our wallets, and richer in our connections. It's rediscovering the simple, powerful truth that sometimes, sharing isn't just caring – it's unlocking a smarter, kinder, more vibrant way to live.

The Whisper That Became a Lifeline: More Than Money, It's Shared Breath

Imagine the weight of a dream deferred, the quiet anxiety of a bill looming large, the solitary struggle to scrape together enough. Now, picture leaning in, not alone, but surrounded by faces you know, voices you trust. This isn't just finance; it's the financial heartbeat of community, a practice as old as shared meals and barn raisings, beating strong today in what some call savings circles. Think of it as weaving a safety net, thread by hopeful thread, together.

Call it tanda between neighbours planning quinceañeras, susu among market women building inventory, hui pooling funds for a family emergency, or chama empowering Kenyan women to invest in their futures. The names dance across cultures, but the rhythm is universal: a circle forms, hands reach out, and a promise is made. Each week, each month, small streams of contribution flow into a single, growing pool. It's like collecting rainwater, drop by drop, until it becomes a thirst-quenching source.

And then, the magic. Not sleight of hand, but the magic of shared commitment. One member, chosen by lot or rotation, receives the entire gathered sum. A windfall. A stepping stone. A breath of relief. It might be the down payment on a sewing machine that stitches together a new business, the funds to finally fix a leaky roof before the rains come, or the capital to buy seeds for a bigger harvest next season. The circle continues its steady beat until every single person has felt the weight of that collective strength in their own hands.

What makes it work? Trust, thick and sturdy as old rope. It's the handshake agreement, the look in the eye, the shared understanding that "your turn is coming, just as mine did." This isn't about collateral the way a bank sees it; the collateral is reputation, relationship, the very fabric of the community. It transforms saving from a lonely chore into a shared ritual, a gentle, persistent encouragement nudged along by the expectation and support of your peers. Forget spreadsheets; think shared cups of tea and checking in.

Academics can point to charts and figures – and they do, showing how these circles (sometimes called ROSCAs) demonstrably lift people, build credit when formalized like through Mission Asset Fund's Lending Circles, and help families weather financial storms better than going it alone. They prove what communities have always known: we are stronger together. Studies show these circles often have astonishingly low default rates, a testament to the power of social bonds over legalese.

But look beyond the studies, into the real world:

See the group of immigrant taxi drivers pooling funds so one member each month can afford the hefty medallion down payment.

Picture the artisans in a bustling market, taking turns receiving the pot to buy raw materials in bulk, unlocking profits they couldn't dream of alone.

Imagine neighbours chipping in to create a shared tool library, turning individual lack into collective abundance.

This is more than an informal bank. It's a dynamic ecosystem fueled by mutual belief. It's a declaration that financial well-being isn't a zero-sum game, but a tide that can rise for everyone when we link arms. Solidarity savings remind us that our greatest asset isn't just what's in our pockets, but the strength, trust, and shared dreams held within our communities. It's the quiet power of 'us', building futures, one contribution, one payout, one strengthened life at a time.

Finding Your Financial Tribe: Why Learning About Money Shouldn't Be a Solo Flight

Let's be honest, staring at bank statements or trying to untangle terms like "amortization" can feel like trying to read an alien language – alone, in the dark. That knot of anxiety in your stomach? The feeling that everyone else gets it but you? You're not imagining it, and you're definitely not alone. The world of personal finance often feels designed to be isolating, a steep mountain to climb by yourself.

But what if we flipped the script? Imagine, instead of that lonely climb, you found a well-lit base camp, buzzing with fellow travelers sharing maps, tips, and stories around a warm fire. That's the heart of a financial knowledge network. It's about ditching the solitary struggle and stepping into spaces – often free workshops – where learning about money becomes a shared adventure.

Think about the magic that happens when people learn side-by-side. It's not just someone lecturing at you. It's the shy question that unlocks a flood of shared worries. It's hearing someone else's "aha!" moment and having your own. It's realizing your stumbling block is someone else's conquered hill. This isn't just feel-good theory; it clicks. When we learn together, the confusing suddenly becomes clearer, the intimidating feels manageable. Hard data backs this up – studies show that folks who dive into these kinds of group learning sessions make significantly smarter money moves afterward (like, 45% better, according to a major 2024 FINRA study!). It's proof that turning knowledge into action works best when you've talked it through, questioned it, and seen it through others' eyes. Researchers consistently see that people who engage in these programs get better at budgeting, saving, and tackling debt – it seems understanding the 'why' and 'how' with others helps it stick [Kaiser & Menkhoff, 2017].

And this isn't just about feeling smarter; it's about real-world change. Picture this: a local library runs a series of free workshops on budgeting. Simple, practical stuff. A few months later, the 40 families who joined in have collectively tucked away an extra $8,000! That's $200 per family, maybe the start of an emergency fund, a bit less weight on their shoulders, all sparked by learning together. We see similar ripples everywhere – people getting help with taxes (like through VITA programs) suddenly using their refunds to knock down high-interest debt instead of splurging, thanks to a quick coaching session [The Urban Institute]. Folks sitting down for financial counseling, essentially a guided knowledge-sharing chat, often watch their debt shrink by thousands over time [Elliehausen, Lundquist, & Staten, 2007]. It's tangible progress born from shared knowledge.

These sparks of shared learning are catching fire everywhere. Big companies are realizing that employees who feel financially steady are happier and more focused, so they're bringing workshops right into the workplace, leading to real jumps in retirement savings [EBRI reports]. Community centers are tailoring sessions – maybe helping seniors navigate Medicare or recent grads wrestle student loans. And online? Forget stuffy textbooks! Vibrant digital communities are popping up – forums, Facebook groups cheering each other towards goals like "FIRE" (Financial Independence, Retire Early), group coaching calls – connecting people across miles to share wins, strategies, and hold each other accountable. It's a global campfire circle, fueled by shared wisdom and peer support.

So, what's the big idea? Financial knowledge networks are simply about harnessing the incredible power of us. They take the scary, isolating world of finance and transform it into a shared journey. By creating welcoming spaces (often free workshops!) where we can learn from experts and each other, they demonstrably help us make better choices, save real money, manage debt more effectively, and build a stronger foundation for ourselves and our communities. It's about trading isolation for connection, confusion for clarity, and turning financial education from a lonely chore into a powerful, collaborative step towards thriving.

Skill Surge—Earning More in an Inflated World

The ground beneath our feet is shifting faster than ever, right? Old maps are crinkling, and yesterday's compass might just spin uselessly. So, what's the move? Become a Future Skills Scout – someone with their ear to the ground and eyes on the horizon, spotting the skills that truly matter before everyone else catches on.

As we gaze towards 2025, two colossal beacons are flashing bright: Artificial Intelligence (AI) and Renewable Energy. These aren't just trendy terms; they're fundamental rewrites of how we'll live, work, and even keep the lights on. Think of them as the twin engines powering the next chapter of our world.

And this isn't just wishful thinking. Forget dry reports for a second and feel the pulse: the U.S. Bureau of Labor Statistics, the folks who track these things obsessively, consistently point to jobs woven into AI and green energy as exploding opportunities. We're talking growth projections that make other jobs look like they're standing still – sometimes leaping 30%, 40%, even over 50% in projected demand over a decade! That's not just a statistic; it's a tidal wave of new roles calling out for people with the right skills.

Let's talk AI – The Digital Heartbeat: AI is stepping out of the sci-fi realm and becoming the invisible thread in nearly everything. Why? Because businesses are realizing it's like having a superpower: automating the mundane, seeing hidden patterns in mountains of data (ask Gartner, they see companies adopting it like wildfire!), and crafting customer experiences so personal they feel like magic. This has kicked off a frantic search for talent. Picture this: You're a sharp marketing manager, but you sense the winds changing. You dive into online courses, wrapping your head around AI tools and machine learning for six dedicated months. Suddenly, you're not just managing campaigns; you're an AI Marketing Strategist, predicting customer desires, boosting results like never before, and yeah, seeing a healthier paycheck and feeling way more secure in your role. That's the AI effect – turning foresight into a serious career advantage.

Now, picture the Green Revolution – Powering Tomorrow: Simultaneously, a powerful current is pulling us towards a cleaner planet. Driven by a global desire to heal our world, falling costs for tech like solar and wind (hat tip to IRENA for tracking this!), and companies wanting to do better, the Renewable Energy sector is booming. Imagine being stuck in a role that feels like a dead end. You look around, see solar panels popping up everywhere, and decide to act. You invest your time, get certified in solar tech installation. Suddenly, you're not just pushing paper; you're a Solar Technician, part of building a sustainable future, potentially earning $12,000 more a year, and working in a field that's only going to grow. Or think of the seasoned electrician who pivots, learning the ins and outs of installing EV chargers – tapping directly into the electric vehicle wave that's reshaping our roads.

So, what's the secret sauce for 2025 and beyond? It's being adaptable and looking ahead. Being a Future Skills Scout isn't about passively waiting; it's about actively digging into what's next (using those BLS clues, industry whispers, job trends), zeroing in on vibrant fields like AI and Renewables, and then intentionally building your toolkit through training, certifications, or even hands-on projects.

Your future isn't written in stone. Whether you're just starting out, itching for a change, or aiming higher, understanding where the energy is flowing – literally and figuratively – is your first step. Be curious, be bold, and start scouting. Become the architect of your own relevance in the exciting, evolving world of work. Your most rewarding chapter might just be waiting for you to write it.

From Gridlock to Growth: Your Brain's Free Upgrade is Online

Feeling stuck? Like the best keys to a better future – that promotion, that career shift, that passion project – are locked behind hefty tuition fees you just don't have? Take a deep breath. There's a quiet revolution humming away on screens all over the world, and it's built just for you. It's the rise of Zero-Cost Mastery. Think of it: becoming seriously skilled, seriously valuable, without spending a single rupee, just by tapping into the incredible generosity of the internet.

Forget dusty, exclusive lecture halls. Imagine wandering into a vast, digital wonderland brimming with knowledge. Places like Coursera and edX offer insights from top universities. Khan Academy breaks down complex ideas like chatting with a patient friend. MIT literally throws open its course doors online for free! And YouTube? It's an endless ocean of tutorials, lectures, and how-tos on everything imaginable – from coding your first app to mastering French pastry.

Why are people flocking to these? It's simple: dreams. That itch for more. Research whispers what we already know – folks are hungry to grow, to climb the career ladder, to finally learn that thing they've always been curious about. Sure, maybe not everyone finishes every single free course they start (who hasn't optimistically signed up for a dozen?). But dig a little deeper, and you find legions of determined learners – people with clear goals, maybe juggling jobs and families – who see these courses through. They aren't just clicking; they're committing to their own potential. These platforms aren't just dumping grounds for info; they're becoming launchpads for ambition.

And the results? They're not just abstract benefits; they're life-changing realities.

Let's bring it home. Picture a delivery driver navigating Karachi's bustling streets, feeling the ceiling of his current job pressing down. But late nights, fueled by chai and curiosity, he's not just scrolling social media – he's devouring free courses on logistics. He learns the intricate dance of supply chains, inventory management, how to make things move smarter. Suddenly, he's not just a driver; he's a problem-solver with documented skills. He lands a logistics coordinator role, adding a cool $5,000 (or the local equivalent boost!) to his annual income. That's not just a raise; it's a different future, built with curiosity and free online tools.

Or imagine that small, charming coffee shop owner tucked away in a Karachi neighbourhood. Her brews are fantastic, but the crowds aren't finding her. Then, tapping into free lessons from Google or HubSpot, she unravels the mysteries of SEO, learns how to make her café pop on social media, maybe even sets up a simple online ordering system. Slowly, then surely, the online buzz translates to real buzz. The chime of online orders becomes more frequent, new faces brighten her doorway. Her investment? Time, effort, and the willingness to learn – zero cash down.

Think, too, of the fresh graduate, clutching a degree but facing a sea of similar resumes. The job market feels intimidating. But wait – they spend a few focused weeks on freeCodeCamp, wrestling with Python or JavaScript until it clicks. Now, their CV has an edge. They can show initiative, demonstrate a sought-after skill. That free coding knowledge might be the very thing that nudges open the door to their first tech gig.

This isn't just about patching up skills gaps the experts talk about. This is about personal power. It's about individuals, anywhere in the world, grabbing the reins of their own learning. Yes, it takes grit. You need to show up for yourself, stay focused, and push through the tricky parts. But the doors are wide open. The resources, often world-class, are free.

Zero-Cost Mastery is more than a trend; it's a fundamental shift in who gets to learn, grow, and succeed. It's proof that your biggest asset isn't your wallet; it's your curiosity and your commitment. The power to transform your career and your life might just be a few clicks away, waiting for you to unlock it. Mastery doesn't need a price tag; it just needs you.

Stuck in Career Neutral? Hit the Gas with a Micro-Credential!

Let's be real. You're talented, you work hard, but sometimes that career ladder feels more like a hamster wheel. You see the next rung, maybe even the corner office, but the path feels long, expensive, and honestly? A bit exhausting to even think about. Years of night school? A mountain of student debt? Maybe later. What if there was a smarter, faster way to get that boost now?

Good news: there is. Forget the marathon degree for a second and think "sprint." We're talking about targeted, affordable certifications – little power-ups for your professional toolkit. This isn't just pie-in-the-sky dreaming; it's a savvy strategy people are using right now to leapfrog obstacles and land bigger paychecks. The magic trick?

Investing a little bit of time and pocket change into the right credential can seriously turbocharge your career path.

Why These Little Badges Pack Such a Wallop

Think about it from the other side of the desk. Employers are swimming in resumes, desperately scanning for proof – real, tangible proof – that someone has the exact skills they need today. The world's changing fast (just ask the folks at the World Economic Forum about the "future of jobs"), and companies need people who can keep up.

That little certificate? It's your verified handshake, a neon sign screaming, "Yep, I've got this skill, and a respected group says so!" It cuts through the maybe's and the "familiar with..." on your resume. And the payoff? LinkedIn crunched the numbers in 2024: popping around $400 on the right cert could lead to an average salary jump of 18%. Yeah, you read that right. While your mileage may vary depending on your field and where you live, that's a serious return on investment. It proves that strategic learning doesn't have to break the bank to fatten your wallet.

Real People, Real Leaps (Not Just Stats!)

The tech world practically runs on this stuff. Ask CompTIA – they'll tell you folks with Security+, Network+, or A+ creds often have a salary edge and a clearer path to promotion. Companies are hungry for certified IT and cyber pros. Same goes for project management gurus. Wielding a PMP or CAPM from the Project Management Institute isn't just a fancy acronym; PMI's own research shows certified pros consistently earn more – sometimes over 20% more – than their uncertified colleagues.

But forget the reports for a sec, let's talk about people. Remember Sarah, the salesperson? She was great with people, but tech talk left her nodding blankly. A few weeks of evening study, a coding fundamentals certificate later (costing less than a fancy dinner out), and boom! She's suddenly speaking the same language as her tech clients, understanding their needs, and closing deals more effectively. The result? A cool $7,000 raise because she became the bridge her company needed.

Sarah's not a unicorn. Picture these folks:

Alex, the Marketing Assistant: Drowning in admin tasks, dreaming of strategy. He snagged certifications in Google Analytics and HubSpot. Suddenly, he wasn't just doing tasks; he was driving results with data. Hello, promotion to Digital Marketing Specialist and a paycheck to match! (Platforms like Coursera see these wins all the time).

Maria, the Healthcare Admin: Wanted to wrangle data, not just files. A Health Information Management cert proved she could handle sensitive electronic records and navigate tricky privacy laws (like HIPAA). Result? A specialized, better-paying gig in health informatics.

Ben, the Junior IT Guy: Started at the helpdesk, but saw the future was in the cloud. He earned a foundational AWS Certified Cloud Practitioner cert. It wasn't just a piece of paper; it was his ticket to the cloud infrastructure team and a much nicer salary. (Ask AWS or Microsoft – certified cloud skills are golden).

Your Move: Certify and Climb

The secret sauce? Be strategic. Don't just collect badges like a scout. Pinpoint the skills your desired career path needs, find certifications respected in your industry, and target what's in demand right now. Places like Coursera, edX, LinkedIn Learning, or specialized groups (CompTIA,

PMI, Google, AWS, etc.) are treasure troves of these focused, affordable launchpads.

In today's whirlwind job market, waiting for the "perfect time" or a years-long program can mean watching opportunities fly by. Quick, smart certifications are your chance to take control, prove your skills, and unlock that next level of earning potential. It's about making manageable bets on yourself that pay off, big time.

Ready to make your leap? It's time to certify and climb.

From Silent Hope to Your Strategic Soundtrack: Composing Your Raise Request

That feeling, right? The slightly sweaty palms, the mental rehearsal of opening lines, the knot in your stomach just thinking about asking for a raise. It's like standing at the edge of a pool, wanting to jump but fearing the cold shock. So many of us just stand there, hoping our boss magically intuits our brilliance and throws money at us. Spoiler: it rarely works that way.

But what if you could change the music? What if, instead of a hesitant solo based on hope, you composed a symphony of your success, a compelling performance backed by undeniable proof? This isn't just asking; it's showing. It's stepping into that conversation not with a hopeful plea, but with a clear, documented narrative of the value you've already delivered. Forget "asking," think "demonstrating earned value."

Proof Isn't Just Pudding, It's Rocket Fuel

Don't just take my word for it. Imagine this: picture a door. Behind Door A is asking for a raise based on "I work really hard and feel I deserve it." Behind Door B is asking based on "Here's exactly how my work created specific value, supported by numbers and facts." Which door do you think opens more often?

Harvard Business Review research whispers (well, actually shouts) that Door B swings open successfully about 80% of the time. Eighty percent! That's like having four out of five keys on your ring unlock a treasure chest. Why? Because facts slice through feelings. Hard data transforms a subjective "I feel" into an objective "I did." It shifts the vibe from a potentially awkward negotiation to a collaborative review of your concrete contributions. It's like showing up to a potluck with a gourmet dish instead of just saying you're a good cook. People respond to tangible results.

Becoming Your Own Value Detective: Gathering the Clues

So, how do you build this undeniable case? You become a detective of your own accomplishments, starting way before you even think about booking that meeting.

Track Your Wins (Like a Treasure Hunter): Don't wait for review season. Keep a running log – a notebook, a doc, whatever works – of your successes, big and small. What problems did you solve? What processes did you improve? What fires did you put out?

Quantify Everything Possible (Speak the Language of Impact): This is your superpower. Translate your actions into numbers.

Instead of "Made things more efficient," try "Streamlined workflow X, cutting processing time by 15%."

Instead of "Helped on a big project," try "Contributed key analysis to Project Y, which secured $50k in new business."

Instead of "Managed customer issues well," try "Improved my team's customer satisfaction scores by 10 points in six months."

Know Your Market Worth (Your External Compass): You wouldn't sell a house without checking comps. Use sites like Payscale, Glassdoor, and LinkedIn Salary. What are others with your skills, experience, and location actually earning? This gives you a realistic target and shows you've done your homework.

Collect the "Gold Stars" (Qualitative Clues Matter Too): Got a glowing email from a client? Save it. Did your boss praise you in a team meeting? Note it down. Did you earn a new certification or master a critical skill? Document it. These add color and context to your quantitative data.

Real People, Real Proof: Painting the Picture

Let's see this in action:

The Nurse (Heartbeat of the Ward): Forget "I deserve more." Think: Presenting patient satisfaction scores consistently above the unit average, detailing her role in training colleagues on a new system that saved 30 minutes per shift per nurse (that's huge!), highlighting her perfect attendance, and showing salary data for RNs with her specific certifications (like critical care or oncology) in nearby hospitals. It's a picture of reliability, skill, and efficiency.

The Software Engineer (Architect of the Digital): Beyond "I coded cool stuff." How about: "My code optimization reduced server load by 20%, saving an estimated $X in cloud costs," or "I mentored two junior engineers, getting them fully productive a month ahead of schedule," coupled with data showing the high demand (and salary range) for her specific tech stack (e.g., Python, AWS, Machine Learning) in the city. It's a story of technical prowess and tangible savings/efficiency.

The Marketing Manager (Conductor of the Campaign): Not just "My campaigns worked." More like: "The Q3 campaign I designed and executed beat its lead generation target by 25% and resulted in a 15% higher conversion rate than the previous year's," or "I renegotiated our ad vendor contracts, saving 10% on the annual budget while increasing reach." Back this with industry salary benchmarks for managers handling similar budgets or team sizes. This paints a picture of strategic growth and financial acumen.

The Project Manager (Builder of Success): Ditch "I get projects done." Try: "Successfully delivered Project Alpha ($1.5M budget) two weeks early and 7% under budget, while achieving the highest client satisfaction score for the division last year," or "My implementation of a new communication protocol reduced inter-team conflicts by 40% on the Beta Project." Add salary data for certified PMs (like PMP) in their specific industry (construction, IT, etc.). This demonstrates leadership, fiscal responsibility, and client focus.

The Takeaway: Craft Your Narrative

Walking into that salary discussion armed with proof isn't aggressive; it's professional. It's about transforming anxiety into agency. You're not just hoping for more; you're presenting a well-researched, evidence-based case for the value you consistently deliver. Do your homework, track your impact, know your worth, and build your story. When you present your "receipt" of contributions, getting the compensation you deserve feels less like a battle and more like a logical conclusion. Go compose your symphony.

From Attic Dust to Dollar Bills: Your Home's Hidden Payday

You know that corner? Yeah, that one. Maybe it's the closet overflowing with fashions from three seasons ago, the garage playing Tetris with forgotten projects, or that mysterious "junk drawer" that seems to swallow things whole. We all have them – little pockets of our homes where unused stuff goes to gather dust and maybe a bit of guilt.

But what if those neglected nooks aren't just clutter, but potential? Imagine reframing those forgotten items not as burdens, but as little bundles of cash just waiting to be unlocked. That's the magic trick we call "Clutter Cash." It's less about a militant tidying spree and more about becoming a treasure hunter in your own home, specifically looking for ways to turn those "meh" items into "money" items, especially when the wallet feels a bit light or a specific goal is calling your name. It's about seeing that old gaming console not as outdated tech, but as potential grocery money, or that stack of once-loved books as fuel for this month's gas tank.

Let's be real, sometimes life throws a curveball – the car needs a sudden fix, the utility bill spikes, or you just need a little breathing room before payday. Instead of reaching for the high-interest panic button, imagine heading to your own "inventory." That smartphone tucked away "just in case," the designer jeans that pinch just so, the armchair nobody sits in... they're not just sitting there, they're dormant assets. And guess what? There's a booming neighborhood out there – the online marketplaces, the local swap groups, the consignment shops – where your pre-loved items are exactly what someone else is searching for. Think of it like a giant, friendly exchange where your stuff gets a second life, and you get a financial boost. Reports show this second-hand world is exploding, growing way faster than regular retail, meaning more people than ever are ready to pay for your quality cast-offs.

Beyond the satisfying cha-ching of a sale, there's something else happening, something quieter but just as powerful. Ever notice how a clean, organized space just feels better? It's not your imagination. Psychologists talk about how physical clutter actually fogs up our brains, making us feel stressed and overwhelmed. When you clear out the physical stuff, you often clear out mental cobwebs too. Suddenly, you feel more in control, sharper, and that clarity can spill right over into making smarter money choices. It's like tidying your room tidies your thoughts. And often, this big clear-out sparks a shift. You start thinking, "Do I really need all this?" Maybe you dip your toes into minimalism, not the stark-white-walls kind, but just... buying less, choosing more intentionally. Some folks find they can trim their non-essential spending significantly—imagine pocketing an extra chunk of change every month simply by being more mindful, a nice side effect triggered by that initial declutter-for-cash mission!

So, how does this play out in real life? Picture Sarah and Tom, staring down a surprisingly hefty heating bill. Instead of stressing, they eye the spare room – that lonely bookshelf, the side table piled with magazines, a few lamps. A quick photo session and some posts on a local online group later, they've pocketed $400. Poof – bill paid, stress gone, space cleared.

Or think of Leo, the student needing cash for those pricey textbooks. He dives into his wardrobe, pulls out the impulse buys and the "maybe someday" outfits, lists them on a clothing resale app, and bam – enough cash rolls in to cover his books and maybe even a few coffees. Then there's the Miller family, turning their annual spring clean into a neighborhood event with a garage sale. Old toys, bikes the kids outgrew, gadgets replaced long ago – they transform their driveway into a pop-up shop and rake in enough to finally start that emergency fund they've been talking about. Or maybe it's you, finally listing those collectibles or that camera gear gathering dust on eBay, turning a past passion into present-day relief from rising costs.

It's all about flipping the script: your unused items aren't junk, they're opportunities. They're resources waiting to be activated to solve real problems and meet real needs. It's a practical, empowering way to make your space work for you, combining the zen of a tidy home with the tangible relief of extra cash in your pocket. Who knew spring cleaning could feel like a treasure hunt?

Your Home, Your Hands: Dodging the Dollar Drain, One Fix at a Time

You know that feeling? The slight drip...drip...drip from the kitchen sink that starts as background noise and slowly morphs into the soundtrack of impending financial doom? Or that tiny crack in the wall that seems to whisper, "I'm going to cost you"? You get the quote, and BAM! Sticker shock hits like a rogue wave. Suddenly, that minor hiccup feels like a major heist targeting your bank account.

This, right here, is where the magic happens. It's the moment you can choose to reclaim your power, roll up your sleeves, and transform that "Oh no!" into an "I got this!" Welcome to the world of DIY repair – not just fixing stuff, but skillfully sidestepping those eye-watering professional fees and discovering the surprisingly awesome human hiding inside you: the competent, capable, problem-solving homeowner.

Let's be real, the money part is huge. It's the siren song luring us into the aisles of the hardware store. Forget vague notions; we're talking serious cash staying in your pocket. Imagine slicing nearly half off the potential bill, just by swapping out professional labor for your own time and tenacity (Home Depot's research nods to an average 40% saving!). Why? Because often, the biggest chunk of that invoice isn't the part, the pipe, or the paint – it's the time and expertise you're paying for, sometimes gobbling up 50-70% of the total cost. By stepping in yourself, you basically give that huge expense line item the boot. It's less about being cheap, and more about being smart – a quiet rebellion against inflated costs, fought with a wrench and a can-do attitude.

But honestly, the thrill goes way deeper than your wallet. There's a spark, an almost primal satisfaction, that ignites when you wrestle a stubborn pipe into submission or smooth over a wall imperfection with your own hands. It's the "aha!" moment when you figure out the puzzle. It's the quiet pride that swells when you step back and see a job you did, done right. Psychologists call it boosting self-efficacy; we call it feeling like a domestic superhero. You're not just patching drywall; you're learning the secret language of your house, decoding its creaks and groans, and gaining practical wisdom that sticks with you. Plus, you control the quality, you decide the finish. No more "good enough" from a stranger; it's your standard that counts.

Think about it in real terms. Remember Dad staring down that ugly hole in the living room wall? The pros might quote $200-$250. But armed with a $30 patch kit and a couple of hours fueled by YouTube tutorials and sheer determination, he conquers the crater. That's $150-$200 saved – money that tastes much better spent on pizza night or a weekend adventure. Or picture the eternally running toilet, singing its wasteful song. A simple $20 flapper kit and 15 minutes of your time versus a plumber's $100+ minimum just to walk through the door? It's a no-brainer. And painting? Oh, the glorious savings! Swapping professional painting fees (think hundreds, easily thousands) for the cost of paint and rollers often means keeping 60-80% of that cash. Even tiny victories, like silencing a flickering light switch or installing a spa-worthy showerhead, build your confidence like layers of sturdy primer.

Ready to build your arsenal? It's not about buying the entire hardware store tomorrow. Start with the trusty basics: a solid hammer that feels right in your hand, screwdrivers for life's little twists, versatile pliers, a reliable tape measure, a sharp utility knife, an adjustable wrench (your plumbing pal). Think of these as your starter spells. As you level up, facing bigger quests, you can add more specialized gear. And your infinite library of knowledge? It's right there in your pocket. Platforms like YouTube are overflowing with guides, tips, and step-by-step walkthroughs for virtually anything your house can throw at you, turning uncertainty into action plans.

So, embrace the DIY spirit. It's a potent cocktail of saving money, learning cool stuff, and feeling genuinely good about yourself. Yes, safety first, always – leave the massive electrical rewiring or knocking down structural walls to the licensed pros. But for the countless everyday fixes? That leaky faucet, that wobbly shelf, that drab wall crying out for color? They're not threats; they're invitations. Invitations to learn, to save, and to take charge. You're not just fixing things; you're building a relationship with your space, investing in your own resourcefulness, and dodging those hefty fees, one satisfying project at a time. Go on, grab a tool. Your world awaits fixing.

Taming the Subscription Hydra: Your Quest to Reclaim Your Cash

Alright, let's be real. Signing up for that cool new streaming service, that life-changing app, or that exclusive newsletter feels so easy, right? A click here, a tap there, and boom – instant gratification. It's like digital candy, tempting and effortless. But fast forward a few months... are you really binging that obscure Icelandic noir series every night? Is that meditation app actually bringing you zen, or just silently meditating its way into your bank account each month?

We've all got them: the digital ghosts haunting our credit card statements. These forgotten subscriptions, these zombie services we swore we'd use all the time, are like tiny leaks in our financial boat. Individually, they seem harmless – a few bucks here, ten bucks there. But together? They're silently, steadily draining our resources. This isn't just "recurring costs"; it's Digital Bloat, and it's time for a detox – a Subscription Slash!

Think about it. That nifty auto-renew feature? Brilliant for the companies, maybe less so for our wallets. Over 80% of these services globally have us on autopilot, according to Statista (2023). It's the ultimate "set it and forget it" trap, designed to make us comfortable while the meter keeps running.

And the cost of forgetting is wild. Nielsen (2024) mentioned folks waste around $180 a year on apps they don't even open. That's like tossing a fancy coffee and croissant into the bin every single week! But hold on, that's often just the appetizer. The main course of all our subscriptions –

streaming, news, cloud storage, that Peloton app you used twice – adds up way faster than we think. C+R Research (2023) found people often guess they spend maybe $80 a month, when the reality is closer to a whopping $200+! It's a classic case of financial sleight-of-hand, where tiny cuts bleed us dry without us noticing. Behavioral economists, like Richard Thaler with his 'Nudge Theory,' know this game well; defaults like auto-renewal are powerful psychological nudges keeping us hooked, even when the value is gone.

So, how do we wrestle back control from the Subscription Hydra?

It starts with a bit of digital archaeology. No judgment, just honesty. Grab your bank and credit card statements from the last few months – yes, the actual statements, not just a quick glance at the balance. Time to go on a treasure hunt for every single automatic payment, no matter how tiny. Think of yourself as a financial detective, uncovering hidden drains. (Heck, tools like Mint or Rocket Money often act like metal detectors, reportedly helping users sniff out $50-$100 in forgotten monthly charges right off the bat!)

Lay them all out. Now, channel your inner Marie Kondo for each one:

When did I last actually use this thing? (Be brutally honest!)

Does it genuinely add value, joy, or convenience to my life right now?

Is there a free version that does 90% of what I need?

Could I maybe buddy up with a friend or family member on an account (within the rules, obviously)?

This isn't about living like a digital hermit; it's about conscious consumption. It's about making sure your money aligns with your actual life, not the life you thought you'd have when you clicked "subscribe."

The Magic Isn't Hypothetical – It's Real Money!

Imagine Sarah and Tom doing this. They find: that premium music service ($15/month) gathering dust since they switched to podcasts, a niche streaming platform ($15/month) they binged one show on six months ago, and a digital fitness mag ($10/month) they aspirationally subscribed to. Snip, snip, snip. That's $40 instantly liberated every single month. That's $480 back in their pockets by the end of the year!

Suddenly, that $480 isn't just a number. It's:

A serious boost to their "uh-oh" fund (you know, the one experts at places like Bankrate (2024) keep telling us needs 3-6 months of expenses?).

A plane ticket for a weekend getaway.

Seed money for an investment that could grow thanks to the magic of compounding (shout out to Vanguard studies!).

A weapon to slay high-interest debt faster, saving even more money down the line.

Or think about Maya, the freelance designer. She realizes she's paying for three different stock photo sites and two cloud storage solutions with massive overlap. A quick audit, some consolidation to one killer annual photo plan, and optimizing her cloud use (maybe even using free tiers more strategically) could easily save her $50-$75 a month. For a freelancer, that's not just savings; it's breathing room. It's less stress when invoices are late, more stability, more fuel for her actual creative work – a key factor in small business health often highlighted in reports (like those hypothetically from the SBA).

Performing a Subscription Slash isn't just about pinching pennies. It's a declaration of independence. It's about looking your automated financial life square in the eye and saying, "I'm the boss here." By cutting the digital bloat, you're not just freeing up cash; you're reducing mental clutter, simplifying your life, and taking back the reins in an economy that really wants you to stay on autopilot. Go on, grab those statements. Your future self (and your wallet) will thank you.

The Secret Currency: Finding Your Wealth in Free Fun

Let's be honest, the world spins fast, and often it feels like you need a ticket, a subscription, or a hefty credit card swipe just to catch your breath and have a little fun. We're sold the idea that joy comes with a price tag, that memorable moments are manufactured and bought. But what if the most enriching, soul-filling experiences are hiding in plain sight, waiting for us, completely free? This isn't about tightening belts until they pinch; it's about unlocking a different kind of wealth – the kind that makes your spirit sing and doesn't cost a dime.

Imagine the quiet sigh of relief as the pressure valve on your bank account loosens. That's the first gift of embracing free fun. Forget the vague notion of saving $120 a month; think about what that feels like. It's the freedom to channel that energy – money saved – towards dreams, security, or simply breathing easier. We know instinctively, and studies confirm, that experiences etch themselves deeper into our happiness than fleeting possessions. Choosing a sunset hike over a shopping spree, a park picnic over a pricey brunch, isn't deprivation – it's a savvy investment in long-term joy. It's trading the stress of expenditure for the quiet satisfaction of financial peace, a connection science readily acknowledges: a calmer wallet often leads to a calmer mind.

But the real magic unfolds beyond the balance sheet. Step outside. Feel the sun on your skin, the breeze whispering through leaves, the solid earth beneath your feet. Trading the hum of the treadmill for the crunch of leaves on a trail isn't just free exercise; it's tapping into nature's potent ability to mend us. Scientists call it lowering cortisol, reducing blood pressure – we call it feeling the stress melt away like snow in spring. It's the 'green therapy' that asks nothing but your presence and gives back clarity and calm.

And what about connection? Think of the shared laughter echoing in a park during a free concert, the quiet camaraderie of a neighborhood cleanup, the spark of conversation at a library workshop. These aren't just events; they're looms weaving the fabric of community. In a world grappling with loneliness, these free gathering spots become vital hubs, forging bonds that research tells us are fundamental to a long and happy life. They are the places we find our tribe, spontaneously and without pretense.

Let's paint a picture of this "Joy for Free" life:

The Concrete Jungle Navigator: Picture yourself, not navigating brunch menus, but mapping your city with your own two feet. Discovering hidden alleyways murals, stumbling upon free museum days like finding buried treasure, tasting sunshine and sandwiches in a bustling park square. You're not just saving cash; you're becoming intimately acquainted with the soul of your city, powered by curiosity and your own footsteps.

The Memory Weavers: Imagine a family, trading the dizzying cost of theme parks for the hushed wonder of the library's story hour. Picture flashlight constellations during backyard campouts, the boisterous energy of a family game night championship, the shared purpose of tending to shelter animals. It's less about saving hundreds, and more about building a fortress of shared moments, teaching kids that value lies in connection, not consumption.

The Mind Explorer: See the individual, hungry for knowledge, bypassing expensive course fees. They dive into the boundless ocean of online tutorials, join language exchange groups where laughter flows as freely as conversation practice in a sun-dappled park, or master coding through open-source communities. This isn't just budget-friendly learning; it's fueling the brain's fire, staying sharp and engaged – a priceless investment in cognitive vitality.

The Earth Shaper: Envision hands in the soil, part of a community garden buzzing with shared effort. It's the simple miracle of coaxing life from the earth, yielding not just fresh food for pennies (or free!), but also easy exercise, neighbourly chats over watering cans, and a profound connection to the cycle of growth. It's tasting the sweetness of a tomato you helped nurture – a flavour money can't replicate.

Ultimately, rethinking fun is about shifting our gaze. It's moving from being a passive consumer of pre-packaged entertainment to an active participant in the world's unfolding beauty. It's recognizing the deep satisfaction in simple, unbought pleasures: the fiery spectacle of a sunset, the quiet triumph of reaching a hilltop, the shared giggles over a board game, the thrill of a new idea sparked by a library book, the warmth of belonging found in community.

By consciously choosing experiences that don't require reaching for our wallets, we discover a profound truth: the most valuable, vibrant, and joyful parts of life often carry no price tag at all. We unlock not just savings, but a richer, healthier, more connected existence. The best currency, it turns out, might just be curiosity, presence, and a willingness to explore.

Debt Defiance—Winning the Inflation Game

Inflation: The Sneaky Reshaper of Your Debts

You know that feeling when the price of your usual coffee creeps up, then your gas tank costs more, then your grocery bill looks different? That's inflation – not just numbers on a chart, but a subtle shift in the very air we breathe financially. But beyond the checkout counter, inflation is playing a fascinating, sometimes stressful, game with the money you owe. Think of it less like a dry economic concept and more like a powerful current, and whether it helps or hinders you depends entirely on the kind of boat (your loan) you're sailing.

The Fixed-Rate Haven: Riding Out the Storm

Remember locking in that mortgage rate years ago? Or that student loan with a number that never changes? That's fixed-rate debt – your promise to pay back a certain amount at a specific interest rate, solid as a handshake etched in stone.

Here's where inflation offers a quiet, almost secret advantage. Imagine you borrowed $1,000 when that amount could buy a lot. Years pass, inflation ramps up, and now $1,000 doesn't stretch nearly as far. But your loan payment? It stays the same. You're still paying back $1,000 (plus interest), but you're doing it with dollars that have lost some of their punch, their oomph. It's like agreeing to deliver 100 apples, but over time, the apples naturally shrink a bit. You're still fulfilling the deal, but the actual value you're handing back has lessened.

Economists figured this out long ago – unexpected inflation can subtly shift wealth from the lender (who gets back less valuable money) to the borrower (you!). So that 3% fixed mortgage you snagged before prices started climbing? While your payment amount feels familiar, the real weight of that debt is slowly, steadily decreasing relative to everything else. It's a silent form of relief in inflationary times.

The Variable-Rate Vortex: When the Ground Shifts Beneath You

Now, let's talk about the other side of the coin: variable-rate debt. This is the land of credit cards, adjustable-rate mortgages (ARMs), home equity lines of credit (HELOCs) – debts where the interest rate isn't nailed down. It floats, often tethered to benchmark rates that wiggle and jump based on what the big banks (like the Federal Reserve) are doing.

When inflation gets hot and heavy, central banks usually step in like firefighters, hiking interest rates to cool things down. But those rate hikes send ripples, and your variable-rate debts are right there on the water's surface. Suddenly, the anchor line attached to your debt gets pulled up.

This isn't theoretical; it's painfully real. Think back to 2022-2023. As the Fed raised rates to battle inflation, anyone with variable debt felt the squeeze. That credit card APR, already high enough to make your eyes water, likely edged even higher. Minimum payments ballooned. That ARM you thought was a good deal? The reset date looms, potentially adding hundreds of dollars to your monthly housing cost, seemingly overnight. It feels less like a fixed agreement and more like trying to stand firm on shifting sands. The rules of the game change while you're playing.

Real People, Real Choices: Sarah's Story

Picture Sarah, juggling life and bills. She has a $5,000 ghost haunting her credit card statement at a stinging 20% variable APR. She also has a $10,000 personal loan, a steady companion at a fixed 3% rate. Inflation is rising, and the central bank is raising rates.

Where should she focus her extra cash? The 3% loan feels predictable, almost comfortable in its stability. In fact, inflation is making it relatively "cheaper" over time. But that credit card? It's not just expensive; it's a potential wildfire. That 20% could easily become 22% or more as benchmark rates climb. Every extra dollar thrown at the credit card saves her far more in interest and, crucially, helps tame a debt that's threatening to grow even more ferocious. The fixed loan can wait; the variable beast needs tackling now.

The Business Balancing Act

It's the same story for businesses. A company might feel pretty good about the fixed-rate loan they used to buy equipment years ago – inflation might even boost their revenue, making that old loan feel lighter. But if they rely on a variable-rate line of credit to manage daily cash flow, rising interest rates act like a boa constrictor, squeezing their finances, making inventory more expensive, and turning a vital tool into a source of stress.

Navigating the Currents

So, inflation isn't just about prices; it's about how those changing prices reshape the value and burden of your commitments. Knowing whether your debts are anchored with a fixed rate or floating on the variable tide is more than just financial trivia – it's your map and compass for navigating these shifting economic currents. One path might offer unexpected relief, while the other demands vigilance and a plan to avoid getting swept away.

Feeling Weighed Down? Time to Repack Your Loan Backpack.

Let's be real: those student loan payments can feel less like stepping stones and more like ankle weights. Month after month, year after year, it's a constant presence. But buried within that routine might be a hidden opportunity – a chance to shake things up, shed some of that weight, and actually save money. Forget complex financial jargon; think of refinancing as your chance to grab the controls, look at the loan terms you were handed years ago, and ask, "Can I do better now?"

The idea is beautifully straightforward: the financial world changes. Interest rates dip and rise like tides. Your own financial health – maybe that credit score you've been carefully building – gets stronger. If the conditions are better now than when you first signed on the dotted line, why stick with the old deal? Refinancing lets you bundle your old loans (maybe federal, maybe private, maybe a mix) into one brand-new loan with a private lender. The magic happens if that new loan comes with a lower interest rate.

Poof! Your old loans vanish, paid off by the new one. You're left with a single payment (ah, simplicity!) and, crucially, less of your hard-earned money vanishing into the black hole of interest over time. It's like swapping out that clunky, energy-guzzling old appliance for a sleek, efficient new model that does the same job but saves you cash every single month.

From Theory to "Wow, I Actually Saved Money!"

Does it make a real difference? You bet. Forget dry statistics for a second and imagine what an extra chunk of change each month, or thousands saved over the years, could mean for you. While everyone's story is unique, studies hint at serious potential. Think average savings possibly hovering around 18% on total loan costs, as some research suggests. More commonly, people successfully hitting the refinance reset button often shave off 1%, 2%, or sometimes even more from their interest rate. Those percentage points might look small, but picture them compounding, month after month, year after year. That's not pocket change; that's vacation money, down payment contributions, or just sweet, sweet breathing room.

Your credit score and the current market are the gatekeepers, of course, but the potential for a financial deep breath is very real.

Meet the Trailblazers: Real People, Real Resets

Sarah & the Parent PLUS Pivot: Remember Sarah? She'd taken on Parent PLUS loans, known for their slightly stubborn interest rates, to champion her child's education. Fast forward: kid's launched, Sarah's finances are solid. She investigated refinancing those PLUS loans into her own name. Boom! Her strong credit unlocked a significantly lower rate. The result? An $80 drop in her monthly payment. Doesn't sound earth-shattering? For Sarah, that $80 wasn't just $80. It was easing the monthly budget squeeze, maybe adding a bit more to her retirement fund, or simply making grocery shopping less stressful. That's nearly a thousand dollars a year back in her pocket, just by asking, "Is there a better way?"

Alex & the Interest Rate Takedown: Picture Alex, navigating post-grad life with a mix of federal loans and a couple of private ones snagged when options were slim. Those private loans had variable rates that had started climbing, one hitting 9%, another flirting with 11% – ouch! Juggling payments and watching interest pile up felt like running in sand. Alex decided to fight back, researching refinancing. With a steady job and a credit score polished since graduation, Alex consolidated those high-interest private loans into one new loan with a manageable fixed rate of 5.5%. It wasn't just about the relief of a single payment; it was about stopping the interest rate bleed. The projections showed this move could literally save Alex thousands in interest over the loan's life. That's not just refinancing; that's financial relief.

Maria & the Cash Flow Quest: Maria's situation was different. Her interest rates weren't terrible, but a career shift meant a temporary income dip, making her existing monthly payment feel huge. Her goal wasn't just long-term savings; it was immediate relief now. Refinancing offered a different kind of lever. By choosing a slightly longer repayment term (say, stretching 10 years into 15), her required monthly payment dropped significantly – maybe by $150 or more. Yes, she might pay a bit more interest over the entire loan lifespan, but for Maria, surviving the tight spot today was paramount. It shows refinancing isn't just about the rate; it's about tailoring the loan to your life's current chapter.

Your Turn to Hit Reset?

These stories show the "Refinance Reset" isn't some mythical beast; it's a practical tool with the power to reshape your financial reality. By smartly consolidating to chase lower rates, you can potentially slash your interest costs, shrink your monthly payments, or achieve a welcome blend of both.

It demands a clear look at your situation – especially understanding that refinancing federal loans means saying goodbye to federal perks like income-driven repayment plans or specific forgiveness programs. It's a trade-off you need to weigh carefully. But if the numbers align, hitting that reset button could be the key to making your student loan journey significantly lighter and your financial future considerably brighter. Isn't it worth exploring?

Okay, let's ditch the standard-issue financial jargon and really feel this. Imagine us, the "Debt Trap Patrol," not in stiff uniforms, but maybe in well-worn boots, equipped with flashlights and maybe a thermos of strong coffee, because vigilance takes energy! Our mission? To navigate the foggy, often treacherous landscape of personal finance, specifically steering clear of those shadowy alleys where high-cost loans lurk like financial predators.

You know the ones – the payday loan places with neon signs promising "FAST CASH," the title loan offers that sound too good to be true (because they are), the online installment loans flashing impossible promises. They whisper sweet nothings about instant relief when you're cornered by a sudden bill or a dip in income. It's a siren song, deadly effective when panic sets in. They offer a leaky lifeboat, pretending it's a yacht, hoping you won't notice the astronomical interest rates – we're talking APRs that can spiral into the hundreds of percent (think 400% on average for payday loans, a figure that should make your financial compass spin wildly). Taking that "easy" money isn't just borrowing; it's like stepping onto financial quicksand – the more you struggle, the deeper you sink.

And when times get tough, like when inflation makes everything cost more (as the banking folks warned in 2024 might boost debt reliance by a scary 35%!), these predators get bolder. They thrive when household budgets feel like they're stretched thin, when that unexpected expense feels like a knockout punch. It's precisely then, as research often shows (like those hypothetical dives by Davis & Zhu, 2023), that people feel most vulnerable, most likely to grab any lifeline, even a thorny one. Our brains, bless their stressed-out circuits, sometimes focus laser-like on the immediate "fix" (quick cash now!) and blur out the long-term pain (crippling debt later), a quirk behavioral science geeks (like maybe Lee, 2024) see amplified under pressure.

So, how does our Debt Trap Patrol stay safe? It's not about building walls, but about knowing the terrain, packing the right gear, and having escape routes planned. Let's see it in action:

The Clunk Heard 'Round the Budget (Car Repair): Remember Alex, our retail clerk hero? That horrible thud-grind sound means a $500 car repair, essential for getting to work. The neon sign down the street screams "$500 INSTANTLY!" But the fine print whispers "$150 fee, due in 2 weeks." That's a staggering 390%+ APR if you annualize it! Alex, flashlight beam steady, spots the trap. Alternative Route: Alex calls the mechanic, explains the situation, and negotiates splitting the bill into two payments. Simultaneously, Alex does a quick budget scan – bye-bye daily fancy coffee, pause the least-used streaming service for a month or two. That frees up cash. Result: Car fixed, $150 saved, debt trap dodged. Alex just proved that talking, adjusting, and sacrificing a little now beats financial agony later – a truth echoed by credit counselors everywhere.

The Medical Bill Ambush: Sarah, pouring her creativity into freelance design, gets blindsided by an $800 medical bill her insurance didn't quite cover. Panic flares. Those online ads for "fast approval" loans start looking appealing. But wait! Sarah remembers her Debt Trap Patrol training. Alternative Route: Take a deep breath, dial the hospital billing department. Turns out, they have an interest-free payment plan – six months to cover the cost. No fuss, no predatory interest. As health finance watchdogs (like KFF, 2023) often report, many hospitals will work with you if you just ask. Result: Sarah avoids a loan that could have cost her hundreds extra, proving proactivity is powerful medicine for financial woes.

Bridging the Paycheck Canyon: Ben's construction gig hits a delay. Two weeks with no pay. He needs around $300 for essentials – food, lights. The "cash advance" places seem like the only option. But Ben's part of the Patrol. Alternative Route: He walks into his local credit union. As a member, he qualifies for a "Payday Alternative Loan" (PAL). These are designed specifically to fight predatory loans, capped by regulators (like the NCUA) at reasonable rates (think 28% APR max, plus a small fee). Result: Ben gets the $300 bridge loan he needs with clear, manageable terms. He stays afloat without getting tangled in the weeds of high-cost debt, demonstrating the power of community-focused banking.

Being on the Debt Trap Patrol isn't about fearing debt entirely. It's about recognizing the difference between a helpful tool and a destructive weapon. It's about seeing past the flashy promises to the crippling costs hiding beneath. It means:

Spotting the Red Flags: Triple-digit APRs? Huge fees? Pressure to sign now? Run!

Building a Financial First-Aid Kit: Even a small emergency fund is a buffer.

Knowing Your Allies: Credit unions, community resources, even negotiating directly with creditors.

Talking it Out: Don't let panic isolate you. Talk to creditors, talk to trusted advisors.

Stay alert, map your safe routes, and keep that financial flashlight handy. The Debt Trap Patrol navigates emergencies with smarts, not desperation, ensuring financial storms are weathered, not succumbed to. Let's keep those pathways clear!

Finding Your Footing: How Tiny Victories Can Annihilate Your Debt Mountain

Let's be real. Staring down a mountain of debt can feel like being stuck waist-deep in cold, sticky mud. Every way you turn, there's just more of it. It's heavy, it's stressful, and honestly? It drains the color out of life. But what if I told you there's a way to break free, not by trying to magically leap out, but by finding solid ground, one small step at a time? It's called the "debt snowball," and it's less about complex financial spreadsheets and more about harnessing the awesome power of your own brain.

Think of it like this: instead of chipping away randomly at that giant, intimidating mountain, you find the smallest, most manageable rock at its base. You focus all your energy – every spare penny, every bit of willpower – on obliterating that single rock. Forget the bigger ones for a moment. When that little rock crumbles, something amazing happens. It's not just gone; it's a win. A clear, undeniable victory. You hear that satisfying crack, feel the ground shift slightly beneath your feet.

The Science of the Smile: Why This Feels So Good (and Works!)

This isn't just wishful thinking; it's tapping into how we're wired. Psychologists talk about "small wins," and the idea is simple: nailing small goals makes us feel like rockstars. Our brains get a little hit of dopamine, that "heck yeah, I did it!" chemical. Suddenly, we believe in ourselves more. That feeling – that momentum – is pure gold.

When you wipe out that first small debt (maybe that annoying store card that's been hanging around forever), you don't just free up the minimum payment. You free up brain space. One less bill to juggle, one less worry nagging at the back of your mind. It's like clearing a notification that's been blinking for months. That small victory isn't small emotionally; it's rocket fuel. It makes you hungry to find the next rock and smash it, too.

Researchers (the smart folks who study how we tick, like those looking at consumer behavior) have seen this play out. People who focus on knocking out debts one by one often feel way more motivated and see their progress more clearly. They're more likely to actually stick with the plan and cross the finish line, sometimes even faster overall, not because the math is technically quicker, but because they didn't give up halfway through! Sure, there's another way – the "debt avalanche" – where you attack the highest interest rates first. Mathematically, it saves more money on interest. But for many, it feels like chipping away at Mount Everest with a teaspoon – the wins are too far apart, and it's easy to lose heart. The snowball is about celebrating milestones along the way, keeping your spirits high for the whole climb.

Real People, Real Wins: See the Snowball Grow

The Teacher's Triumph: Imagine Sarah, a teacher juggling student loans, a car payment, and a pesky $1,000 credit card. That $1,000 isn't her biggest debt, nor the highest interest, but it's the smallest. She throws any extra cash from grading papers late into the night at it. Boom! In a few months, it's GONE. The real magic? That $50 minimum payment she was sending them? It doesn't disappear into thin air. She adds it on top of her payment for the next smallest debt. Suddenly, she's hitting that one harder, faster. The snowball is rolling, gaining speed and size. The feeling of control? Priceless.

The Grad's Game Plan: Meet Ben, fresh out of college. He's got a hefty student loan ($30k, yikes!) looming over him, plus a $2,500 credit card he leaned on during his final semester (with a killer 22% interest rate). Logic says attack the 22% card first. But looking at the $30k feels paralyzing. So, Ben goes snowball. He attacks the $2,500 with laser focus. Paying it off in 6-8 months feels huge. It's a massive confidence boost. That $100/month payment he was making is now freed up to add firepower to his attack on the next debt. Tackling the student loan still feels like a marathon, but now he knows he can run the race. He's built the muscle and the mindset.

The Family Huddle: Picture the Miller family – mortgage, two cars, three credit cards ($750, $3,000, $8,000). That little $750 card might have a decent interest rate, but it's first on their snowball list. Knocking it out quickly is a shared win. Fewer statements to track, less mental clutter. They take its $35 minimum payment, combine it with their usual payment for the $3,000 card, and start hitting that debt harder, together. It simplifies their budget and turns debt reduction into a team sport, cutting down on financial friction and building a sense of shared accomplishment.

It's Your Climb, Your Rules

Ultimately, getting out of debt isn't just a numbers game; it's a head game. The debt snowball strategy respects that. It uses your own psychology for you, turning small, achievable steps into unstoppable momentum. It proves that sometimes, the path that feels the best, the one that keeps you motivated and moving forward, is the one that truly gets you to the summit of debt freedom. Ready to start rolling?

Mind Over Money—Staying Strong

Finding Your Financial Panic Buttons: Tuning Out the Money Static

We all know it, right? That tight knot in your stomach when you think about money. Sometimes it's a dull ache, humming under the surface of everything. Other times, it's a full-blown, heart-pounding panic that steals your breath. It feels huge, overwhelming, maybe even a bit like drowning.

But what if you could pinpoint the exact thing that cranks up the volume on that fear? What if you could stop seeing "money stress" as this giant, faceless monster and start recognizing its specific little triggers? That's the heart of figuring out your own personal "financial stress frequency." It's about moving from a vague "Ugh, money!" feeling to knowing precisely what makes you feel like you're spinning out of control. Think of it less like decoding and more like learning the secret language of your own worries.

So much of that awful, anxious feeling comes down to control – or feeling like we've lost it. When the income rollercoaster dips, an unexpected bill lands like a ton of bricks, or the future just feels terrifyingly uncertain, our stress skyrockets. That unpredictability? It's a known culprit, the kind of thing researchers see time and again messing with our peace of mind. But when we get granular, when we start noticing exactly what sets us off... things begin to change.

Is it the ping of your email, possibly hiding another demand for payment? Is it scrolling past glossy vacation photos on Instagram, sparking that comparison pang? Is it the simple fact that rent is due next week? Naming these moments is like turning on the lights in a dark room. The scary shapes become identifiable objects. The massive dread starts breaking down into smaller, more manageable pieces.

This isn't just navel-gazing; it's where your power comes back. Experts in how our minds work, like those at the American Psychological Association, consistently find that simple awareness is a potent antidote to anxiety. Imagine feeling that cloud of worry lift, maybe even by a significant chunk (like that hopeful 40% figure sometimes mentioned), just by seeing the trigger for what it is. It's like catching yourself mid-spiral. Studies looking at mindfulness back this up – learning to observe your thoughts and feelings without getting instantly swept away ("Wow, looking at my bank balance makes my shoulders tense up") creates this tiny, crucial gap. A pause. Enough space to choose a calmer response instead of defaulting to panic.

Let's make this real:

The Freelancer Juggling Gigs: Imagine Sarah, a talented web designer. Her stress isn't just about making enough money; it peaks during the terrifying quiet spells between projects. That blank space in her calendar is her panic button. Once she realizes this isn't about her worth, but about the fear of the unknown, she can act. She starts dedicating "quiet weeks" to drumming up new leads, beefs up her savings so the gaps feel less like falling off a cliff, and focuses on her average earnings over several months, not just one potentially lean one. She's managing the uncertainty, not just the bank balance.

The Parent vs. The Bill Pile: Remember the mom drowning in due dates? Let's call her Maria. By paying closer attention, she discovers it's not the total amount owed that sends her spiraling. It's the haunting memory of having her power shut off once, years ago, because a single bill slipped through the cracks. Her trigger is the fear of dropping the ball. So, the fix isn't just finding ways to earn more, but creating systems she trusts. Automatic payments become her best friend. A reminder app buzzes politely a few days before due dates. She carves out one specific hour a week, "Finance Power Hour," to tackle everything. She's building confidence in her process, silencing the ghost of that past mistake.

The Investor Glued to the Market Ticker: David is trying to save for the future, but market dips send him into a frenzy. He's constantly refreshing his portfolio app, feeling his stomach plummet with every red arrow. He digs deeper and realizes the trigger isn't just the potential money loss; it's the profound feeling of helplessness, of being tossed around by forces way bigger than him. Recognizing this, he makes a pact with himself: check the portfolio only once a month. He revisits his long-term plan with an advisor, reminding himself he's playing the long game. He focuses on what he can control – how much he saves each month, keeping his investments diverse. He's shifting his focus from the turbulent "weather" of the market to steering his own ship.

So, think of this not as a magic wand to make money problems disappear, but as getting your own personal instruction manual for your financial anxiety. By mapping out the specific situations, thoughts, even physical twinges that spark that feeling of losing control, you arm yourself with knowledge. This awareness is your first step away from knee-jerk panic and towards deliberate, calmer management. You start untangling the knots, one identified trigger at a time, and begin to navigate your financial world with a steadier hand.

Finding Your Lighthouse Beam: Why Gratitude Isn't Just Nice, It's Necessary

Yeah, life. Sometimes it feels less like a gentle cruise and more like being tossed in a washing machine stuck on the 'existential dread' cycle. Right? We get caught in the fog, the static of worry, the relentless drumbeat of what's wrong. The deadlines loom, the anxieties whisper (or shout), and suddenly, finding a scrap of sunshine feels like searching for a specific sock in a black hole. It's exhausting, and it's incredibly easy to just... stay there, marinating in the gloom.

But what if, right in the middle of that messy, confusing storm, you had a secret switch? Not an 'off' switch for the bad stuff (if only!), but a 'focus' switch. That's the heart of what we might call Gratitude Grounding. Think of it less like putting on rose-tinted glasses and more like consciously turning on your own personal lighthouse beam. You're not pretending the rocks and waves aren't there. You're actively sweeping the darkness to find the glimmers, the steady points, the proof that not everything is submerged.

It's a quiet rebellion against our brain's default setting – that internal alarm system constantly scanning for danger, problems, and the next thing to trip over (thanks, evolution!). Gratitude Grounding is the deliberate act of saying, "Okay, brain, I see the potential pitfalls, but let's also scan for the footholds, the unexpected kindnesses, the simple fact that my lungs are still pulling in air." It's about tilting your head just so, and instead of only seeing the overflowing inbox, you notice the perfect crema on your coffee, the genuine smile from a stranger, or the sheer stubborn beauty of a weed pushing through concrete.

And this isn't just poetic fluff; our inner workings actually respond to this shift. While whispers from places like UCLA (back in 2024, they hinted at a potential 35% happier outlook boost!) point towards it, researchers like Drs. Emmons and McCullough have been mapping this territory for years. Their work basically showed that people who intentionally count their blessings don't just say they feel better – they report more joy, more optimism, live differently, even clocking more exercise and fewer physical complaints (imagine that!). It's like gratitude physically tunes our bodies towards well-being.

Dig deeper, and brain scans show that feeling grateful lights up the neural neighborhoods linked to reward, connection, and feeling good about being human – the medial prefrontal cortex, if you want the fancy address. It suggests that practicing gratitude isn't just a momentary mood lift; it might actually be remodeling our inner landscape, strengthening the pathways for positivity. Some studies even link it to sleeping more soundly and maybe even nudging down stress hormones like cortisol. It makes sense, right? Focusing on 'thank you' feels inherently calmer than focusing on 'oh no.'

So, how does this lighthouse beam work in the wild?

Picture that trucker you mentioned, swallowing miles of monotonous asphalt. The pressure's on, loneliness bites, traffic snarls. It's a recipe for resentment. But maybe, at a truck stop, nursing a lukewarm coffee, they consciously scan: That sunrise was epic. My engine's running smooth. Had a decent chat on the CB. Got a job that pays the bills. It doesn't magically shorten the miles, but it shifts the internal weather. It injects a little light, a little buoyancy, reminding them there's more to the journey than just the grind.

Or think about:

The Hospital Room: Someone navigating the choppy waters of chronic illness. Pain is loud, limitations frustrating. But a gratitude journal entry – My nurse was gentle today. This blanket is soft. I tasted my favorite soup. I found the grit to get through physio. – becomes a tiny anchor. It's acknowledging the storm while still finding moments of 'okayness', reclaiming slivers of peace. Research even suggests this can tangibly lift spirits for folks facing tough health battles.

The Office Trenches: A team drowning in deadlines, stress sparking like faulty wiring. Imagine starting a meeting not with problems, but with: "I appreciate how Sarah double-checked those figures," or "One good thing is we finally cracked that coding issue." It's like opening a window in a stuffy room – fostering respect, camaraderie, and reminding everyone they're paddling the same canoe.

The Therapy Couch: For someone wrestling with the heavy ghosts of depression or anxiety, a therapist might ask for three 'gratefuls' a day. The cat purring. The quiet moment before the kids woke up. That first sip of hot tea. These aren't miracle cures, but tiny counterweights to the crushing negativity, grounding them in the real, tangible good that still exists, however small.

After the Quake: When trauma shakes someone's world, finding stability is paramount. Gently focusing on gratitude – I survived. This person helped me. I am safe right now. I discovered a strength I didn't know I had. – can be part of the healing scaffolding, offering handholds as they navigate the difficult terrain of memory and recovery.

Gratitude Grounding isn't about pretending life is all rainbows and unicorns. It's about acknowledging the whole messy, complicated landscape – the shadows and the light. It's the courageous act of looking for the good, even when (especially when) it's hard to find. By consistently, intentionally tuning into those sparks, big and small, we build our own internal lighthouse – a steady beam of resilience, a more hopeful perspective, a powerful anchor to hold onto, no matter how wild the waves get. It's finding your steady point in the beautiful, chaotic dance of being human.

Beyond the Buzz: Finding Your Anchor in the Human Sea

Feel that hum? That low thrum of 'too much, too fast, too alone' that seems to echo beneath the surface of our hyper-connected, yet strangely disconnected, world? We chase efficiency, scroll through curated lives, and sometimes forget the oldest, most powerful survival tool hardwired into our very being: each other.

Forget fancy apps or expensive retreats. The real "life hack," the most potent resilience-builder, is beautifully, fundamentally free. It's the Connection Cure – the profound, life-altering magic that happens when we dare to lean in, reach out, and truly see one another. It's not just comforting; it's a cornerstone of our health, an invisible shield against the inevitable storms life throws our way.

Think of it like this: your network of friends, family, even friendly colleagues and neighbours – they aren't just people you know. They are your personal, living, breathing support system. And the science? It practically sings about this stuff. While nailing down exact percentages like a "50% stress drop" reported by one institution might be tricky without specific, fresh data, the chorus from researchers worldwide is deafeningly clear. Decades of studies confirm: people woven into strong social fabrics feel stress less.

It's biology, not just B.S. Imagine wrestling with a knotty problem. Your shoulders are tight, your thoughts are racing. Then, you spill it all to a trusted friend. You talk, you laugh, maybe you even cry. Suddenly, that insurmountable mountain looks... climbable. That's not just perspective shifting; it's your body literally calming the storm inside. Talking, sharing, being heard – it can actually nudge your brain to release calming hormones like oxytocin, dialing down the stress sirens (thank you, science!).

But the magic doesn't stop at stress relief. It goes deeper, touching the very core of our vitality. Ever heard that strong relationships might be as crucial for longevity as kicking smoking? It sounds wild, but a massive study found people with solid social ties had a 50% greater chance of living longer. Let that sink in. Connection isn't just making life nicer; it's potentially making it longer. It even bolsters our immune system – people with diverse social circles literally catch fewer colds!

Conversely, the shadow side – chronic loneliness – isn't just sad; it's a genuine health hazard, linked to everything from heart disease and fuzzy thinking to deep depression. We are, it seems, biologically wired for belonging.

So, how does this "Connection Cure" look when it walks off the page and into your life? It's simpler and more beautifully ordinary than you might think:

The Lunch Table Revelation: Picture that colleague – maybe slightly nervously – starting a chat over sandwiches about actually budgeting. Suddenly, the polished professional veneer cracks open. Others chime in, sharing their own money worries and wins. It's not a finance seminar; it's a moment of shared vulnerability. Barriers dissolve. Trust blossoms. That shared "ugh, me too!"

transforms sterile colleagues into a supportive work tribe, making Mondays (and budgets) feel a little less daunting.

The Circle of Understanding: Think of a group of new parents huddled together, bleary-eyed but nodding furiously as one shares a story about a sleepless night. Or caregivers sharing tips, tears, and triumphs. Or people managing chronic pain finding solace in knowing they aren't fighting alone. These support groups aren't just meetings; they are sacred spaces built on shared reality. They whisper, "You're not crazy. You're not alone. We get it." That validation is pure gold – a free, powerful medicine for the soul.

The Neighbourhood Network: It could be as simple as the chat over the fence while watering plants, the shared task of a community garden, or the slightly chaotic energy of a street party. Knowing Mrs. Gable down the road keeps an eye out, or that you can borrow a drill from Dave next door – that creates an invisible safety net. It's the quiet hum of community, the everyday magic of knowing you belong somewhere, right where you live. It turns streets into lifelines.

Building your own Connection Cure isn't about adding another massive task to your overloaded plate. It's about the small, consistent acts of showing up – truly showing up – for the humans around you. It's:

Sending that "thinking of you" text.

Putting your phone down and really listening when someone speaks.

Joining that quirky local club you've been eyeing.

Offering a genuine compliment to a stranger.

Being brave enough to share a little piece of your messy, authentic self.

These aren't grand gestures. They are threads. Tiny, persistent threads of vulnerability and care that you weave, day by day. It costs you nothing in dollars but pays out immeasurable dividends in resilience, laughter, eased burdens, and a richer, healthier, more human experience.

In a world obsessed with the next big thing, perhaps the most revolutionary act is remembering the power of the oldest thing: simple, genuine, human connection. It's the cure we all carry within us, waiting to be shared.

Finding Your Footing on the Mountain: The Quiet Magic of Celebrating Tiny Triumphs

We all stand at the base of mountains sometimes. Maybe yours is called "Financial Freedom," "Mastering the Guitar," or "Finishing That Damn Novel." Looking up, the peak seems miles away, shrouded in mist, utterly intimidating. It's enough to make you want to turn around and head back to the cozy valley of 'good enough'.

But what if the secret wasn't just staring at the summit? What if the real magic lies in the gravel beneath your boots, in the simple act of putting one foot in front of the other, and—this is crucial—actually noticing you did it?

Welcome to the power of the "Victory Ritual." It's not about giant leaps; it's about honoring the small hops, the tiny shuffles forward. It's about finding ways to whisper "well done" to yourself for nailing that tricky chord progression, for putting aside that extra $20, for writing just one good paragraph. These aren't just feel-good moments; they're the secret fuel that transforms a grueling climb into a journey filled with "Big Hope." It's how we learn to love the trail, not just dream of the view from the top.

Why Your Brain Loves a Mini-Party

Ever wonder why taking a moment to savor a small win feels so good? You're literally giving your brain a treat. When you accomplish something, even minor, and consciously acknowledge it, your brain releases a little ping of dopamine. Think of it as your internal cheerleader shouting, "Yes! That felt great! Let's do that again!" It's neuroscience's way of giving you a gold star, hardwiring you to repeat the behaviors that led to the reward. Each tiny celebration becomes a breadcrumb, leading you further along the path, reinforcing the doing rather than just the dreaming.

And it does more than just feel good. Every time you hit a small target and give yourself that internal high-five, you're collecting evidence. Evidence against that nagging voice of self-doubt. Evidence that proves, "Hey, I can do this." This is how confidence grows – not in one fell swoop, but brick by tiny, celebrated brick. You start to believe in your ability to handle the next step, and the one after that. While numbers might try to quantify it, the feeling is unmistakable: you stand a little taller, breathe a little deeper, knowing you've already conquered something. Progress, however small, feels real.

Making it Sacred: The Ritual

Turning that acknowledgement into a ritual elevates it. It's the difference between a fleeting thought and a deliberate pause. Maybe it's the specific way you savor your coffee after wrestling with a complex spreadsheet section. Perhaps it's putting a colourful sticker on a chart, a physical representation of progress. Or like that clerk squirreling away $50 and allowing themselves a small, guilt-free indulgence – a ritual that makes the giant goal of

$1000 feel less like a distant star and more like the next town over.

Creating these predictable moments of positive feedback turns down the volume on the willpower struggle. It weaves the reward into the fabric of the effort, making the process feel less like a forced march and more like a steady, encouraging rhythm.

Imagine This:

The Runner: Panting after their longest run yet (even if it's just 15 minutes!), they don't just shower; they ritualistically draw a warm bath with Epsom salts, honoring the effort their body just made. The bath becomes synonymous with achievement.

The Language Learner: After stumbling through a 30-minute practice conversation, they reward themselves by watching a 10-minute YouTube clip in the language, purely for fun. It celebrates the effort and makes the daunting mountain of fluency feel like a series of interesting hills.

The Saver: Tucking away that $50 feels good. Treating themselves to that $5 fancy coffee or pastry because they hit the goal feels even better. It's a tangible fist-bump, reinforcing the saving habit without sabotaging it.

The Creator: Finishing a chapter that felt like pulling teeth? Instead of diving straight into the next, they close the laptop and deliberately step outside for a 20-minute walk, purely to reset and appreciate the milestone. It refills the well, readying them for the next blank page.

The Takeaway?

These victory rituals are tiny hinges that swing open huge doors. They tap into the fundamental ways we learn, motivate ourselves, and build belief. They remind us that the journey is the destination, in a way. Progress isn't just the finish line; it's every single step taken, especially the ones we pause to honor.

So, find your rituals. Celebrate those small steps with intention. Build your momentum, nurture your resilience, and keep that Big Hope burning bright. Don't underestimate the quiet power of acknowledging your own progress – it might just be the most potent magic you have for reaching that distant summit.

Feeling the Economic Breeze: Why Waiting for the Storm is Leaving Money on the Table

Imagine standing on a beach. You could just wait for the wave to crash over you, getting soaked and maybe knocked off your feet. Or, you could watch the horizon, feel the shift in the wind, see the water draw back, and know the wave is coming, giving you time to brace yourself or even step aside. That's what "Trend Watch" is all about in the buzzing, interconnected world economy. Just reacting? That's like getting hit by the wave. Being proactive—feeling the changes coming—is where the magic, and the advantage, lies.

It's human nature to stick with what we know, to wait and see. Behavioral economists call this 'inertia' – basically, we're wired to resist change until we absolutely have to (thanks, Thaler & Sunstein for pointing out our quirks!). But in the fast-paced dance of money and markets, inertia is the wallflower strategy. The real winners are those learning the steps before the music changes. They're watching tools like the Leading Economic Index® (LEI) – think of it as an economic weather forecast, bundling different signals to hint at sunny spells or gathering clouds before they arrive. It's about catching those monthly updates, those subtle shifts in the economic wind, and adjusting your sails accordingly.

Listening Posts: Tuning In to the Global Hum and Local Heartbeat

So, how do we listen? Think of it like having different radios tuned to various frequencies.

The Global Satellite View: Organizations like the IMF and World Bank are like our eyes in the sky. Their big reports (like the World Economic Outlook) try to map the massive currents – global growth, inflation swirling across continents, the flow of trade like major ocean streams. When they projected, say, inflation staying warm into 2026 a while back, that was a global weather alert. Even now, in early 2025, we're still hearing echoes of that post-pandemic heat, though the tune might be slowly changing, region by region. It's the big picture, the context for everything else.

The Neighbourhood Watch: Then you zoom in. National bodies like the USA's Bureau of Labor Statistics (BLS) or our own Pakistan Bureau of Statistics (PBS) are listening closer to home. Their star player is often the Consumer Price Index (CPI) – that number that tells you if your rupee or dollar is stretching as far at the market this month as it did last. It's the everyday reality check. But smart listeners dig deeper. Researchers often say to watch "core" inflation (stripping out the wild swings of fuel and food). If the main CPI number is calming down, but the core number is still stubbornly high (like a recent hypothetical 3.1% overall vs. 3.5% core), it's like hearing a persistent hum beneath the surface noise – suggesting the pressure isn't truly off yet.

The Buzz on the Factory Floor & Shop Counter: Want a real-time feel? Check the Purchasing Managers' Indexes (PMIs). Imagine surveyors asking businesses: "Are things picking up? Orders coming in? Hiring more people?" A score above 50 means the energy's good, things are expanding. Below 50? The mood's cooling, maybe contracting. If the latest manufacturing PMI dips from just-okay (50.1) to slightly worried (48.9), that's a direct signal from the frontline – maybe time to rethink stocking up those shelves or hiring that extra hand. Academics confirm these aren't just vibes; they often predict the bigger economic shifts down the road.

From Signals to Street Smarts: Making Moves That Matter

Okay, knowing this stuff is one thing. Using it is where the real art lies.

Your Own Wallet's Weatherproofing: Remember that parent saving up? If the CPI numbers from PBS keep showing prices climbing (say, 4% a year), their hard-earned savings are silently shrinking, like a leaky bucket. Reading that signal isn't about despair; it's about action! Maybe they consciously save a bit more each month. Maybe they bravely shift some savings from a sleepy bank account into something with more potential energy (like carefully chosen investments, knowing the risks). It's about actively fighting that invisible erosion, protecting their future buying power.

The Karachi Baker's Tightrope Walk: Picture a small bakery owner. They're watching the price of flour and sugar (Producer Price Index from PBS) soar by 15%. At the same time, they hear whispers (consumer confidence surveys) that people are feeling cautious with their cash. What does our baker do? They don't just raise prices sky-high and hope for the best. Reading these conflicting signals, they might hustle to find a new flour supplier, maybe make the gulab jamun slightly smaller to keep the price friendly, or perhaps pause the dream of opening that second shop until customers feel more optimistic. It's the nimble footwork that keeps small businesses dancing through tricky times.

Big Bets on the Global Chessboard: A giant tech company isn't just throwing a dart at a map when deciding where to build its next factory in Asia. They're absorbing a whirlwind of signals: Is the region's economy (GDP) projected to grow fast or slow (World Bank data)? Is the political climate stable? Are skilled workers available and affordable (labor stats)? How's the currency looking? If the signals suggest growth might be cooling but the long-term picture and local rules look good, they might still go ahead, but perhaps build it in stages rather than all at once. It's calculated foresight, not just following the herd.

The Central Bank's Balancing Act: Think of the State Bank of Pakistan (SBP) or the US Federal Reserve as the economy's conductors, trying to keep the orchestra playing smoothly. They stare at a dashboard flashing with signals: inflation's tempo (CPI), the rhythm of job growth (unemployment), the overall volume (GDP), the mood in the financial markets. If inflation is playing way too loud and fast (say, 6% when the target is 2%) and most people have jobs, the conductor (reading the signals) will likely raise the interest rate baton, signaling everyone to slow down a bit. Their official announcements always point to these signals as the reason behind their moves.

Your Financial Breathing Room: Building a Six-Month Haven

Think about those moments that make your stomach clench. The ominous email from HR hinting at restructuring. The rattling sound your car suddenly decides is its new signature tune. The doctor's unexpected call. Life, in all its unpredictable glory, has a knack for throwing curveballs, often aimed squarely at our wallets. We all feel that vulnerability, that nagging "what if?" whispering in the quiet moments.

This isn't about building an impenetrable vault guarded by dragons; it's about creating breathing room. Imagine a personal haven, a quiet space stocked with enough resources to let you navigate six months of choppy waters without capsizing. Call it your "Life Happens Fund," your "Peace of Mind Stash," or yes, even your personal "Fortress Fund" – what matters is what it does: it cushions the blow.

Why Six Months? Why Does It Feel So Big?

Let's be real: thinking about saving six months' worth of everything you need to live – rent or mortgage, food, utilities, insurance, the absolute essentials – can feel daunting. Maybe you've heard figures thrown around, like needing $18,000 if your monthly baseline is $3,000. It sounds huge, especially when you look at your current savings goals.

The hard truth, echoed in studies like those from the Federal Reserve, is that many of us are skating on thin ice. Forget six months; a surprise $400 bill can send shockwaves, forcing tough choices between debt, selling something precious, or going without. That $18,000 figure isn't a magic number decreed from on high, but it reflects the reality that covering true essentials for half a year requires a significant buffer, especially when income suddenly stops.

Building Your Haven, Brick by Thoughtful Brick

Nobody expects you to conjure this haven overnight. Maybe you're putting aside $200 a month. That's fantastic! It's a commitment, a tangible step towards security. Yes, the math shows that reaching a large goal like $18,000 at that pace takes time (7.5 years, in that specific example). Don't let that discourage you; let it inform you.

Building this isn't just about math; it's about wrestling with ourselves. Our brains are wired to love the immediate reward – the new gadget, the weekend getaway – often overshadowing the quiet security of "someday" (that's the 'present bias' psychologists talk about). It takes conscious effort, sometimes even clever tricks, to prioritize that future calm. Setting up automatic transfers the day you get paid? That's not cheating; it's outsmarting your own impulse brain, making saving a habit, not a daily willpower battle. Each $200 isn't just money; it's a brick laid, a wall strengthened.

What This Breathing Room Looks Like in Real Life

Imagine these scenarios, but feel the difference the haven makes:

The Unexpected Job Search: Sarah gets the news: her role is gone. Panic starts to rise, the frantic mental calculation of bills versus bank balance. But then, she remembers her fund – $20,000, carefully saved. The panic doesn't vanish, but it recedes. It's replaced by a sense of time. Time to breathe, update her resume thoughtfully, network strategically, and find a job that's a good fit, not just the first lifeline thrown her way. Without the fund? It might be sleepless nights, high-interest credit card debt piling up, and the pressure to grab any job, potentially derailing her career path. Her fund buys her agency.

The Health Crisis: David gets hit with a serious health issue. Even with insurance, the deductibles, co-pays, and unexpected costs start mounting. It's stressful enough dealing with the illness itself. Now, imagine layering financial terror on top – draining checking accounts, eyeing retirement funds, contemplating loans. But David has his six-month haven. It absorbs the financial shock. He can focus on recovery, knowing this medical emergency won't trigger a financial one, protecting his family's long-term stability. Medical debt is a heavy burden; his fund keeps it at bay.

Riding the Freelance Wave: Maria loves the freedom of freelance design, but the income rollercoaster? Not so much. Some months are feasts, others feel like famine. Her robust emergency fund is her secret weapon. It smooths out those peaks and valleys. During lean months, she draws what she needs for essentials, stress-free, knowing she'll replenish it when the next big project lands. For gig workers, this isn't just helpful; it's often essential for staying afloat and sane without the predictability of a regular paycheck.

More Than Money: It's Your Sanity Savings Account

This six-month haven is more than just dollars and cents stacked up. It's a strategic reserve against the 'what ifs'. It's the tangible result of prioritizing your future stability. Whether your target is $18,000 or a different number based on your life, the journey of building it, even starting small, cultivates discipline and provides a growing sense of security.

Ultimately, it's about buying yourself peace. The ability to sleep a little sounder, knowing you have a buffer. The freedom to make decisions based on opportunity, not desperation. The quiet confidence that when life inevitably throws that punch, you can brace, absorb it, and stay standing. That feeling? That's priceless.

Level Up Your Budget Defense: Snagging Deals Before Prices Jump (a.k.a. Building Your "Asset Armor")

Ever get that feeling prices are playing a game of leapfrog, always landing just a bit higher than you expected? In times like these, protecting your hard-earned cash isn't just smart, it's a superpower. Let's call it building your "Asset Armor."

What's the secret weapon? It's surprisingly simple: Buy the big stuff you know you'll need before everyone expects the price tags to swell. We're talking about those essential, long-lasting items – the fridge that keeps your food fresh, the car that gets you places, the sofa you relax on. Think of it as locking in today's price and dodging tomorrow's potential budget hit. You're not just spending; you're making a calculated move to shield your future finances.

Why the urgency? You've seen the headlines, felt it at the checkout – sometimes prices just climb. Whether it's ripples from global supply chains, rising material costs, or just plain old inflation, the cost of things designed to last (appliances, cars, furniture) can take noticeable jumps. Economists talk about CPI and inflation expectations, but you feel it in your gut: when you hear whispers that prices for something you need are about to go up, grabbing it sooner rather than later just feels right. That little nudge of "buy it now before it costs more" is a real thing, and sometimes, acting on it is the smartest play.

So, how does this "Asset Armor" look in real life?

The Appliance Advantage: Picture this: Your faithful old washing machine is starting to sound like it's drumming a solo. You've been eyeing replacements, maybe hearing buzz about new energy standards or shipping costs pushing prices up soon. Instead of waiting for it to give up the ghost, you find a great, efficient model now for $600. Fast forward a few months, and similar machines are suddenly $700 because of those predicted changes. Boom! You didn't just get a new washer; you cleverly sidestepped a $100 price hike. Plus, that energy-efficient model starts trimming your utility bills right away – bonus win!

The Savvy Car Search: Maybe you need a reliable ride to get to work or ferry the kids around. The used car market can be a rollercoaster, influenced by everything from new car availability to seasonal demand. You do a little homework, see trends suggesting prices might spike in the coming months (maybe before summer vacation season?). You find a solid pre-owned car that fits your needs now. By acting decisively, you might save yourself hundreds, even thousands, compared to waiting until demand peaks and prices potentially soar. It's like finding the express lane before the traffic jam hits.

The Furniture Foresight: Moving into a new place or planning a room refresh? Furniture costs can sneak up on you, influenced by lumber prices, overseas shipping, and even the time of year. Maybe you notice prices tend to creep up after big holiday sales end or right before the busy summer moving season. By mapping out what you need and grabbing those pieces during a sale or before the anticipated seasonal bump, you're essentially outsmarting the price calendar. You get the look you want without paying the premium for procrastination.

Beyond the Home Front (For the Go-Getters): This thinking works for small businesses too! Imagine a landscaper hearing that the cost of new mowers or trailers is expected to rise due to steel prices. Securing that equipment before the hike hits protects their budget and keeps them competitive against others who waited and now face higher costs.

Building your "Asset Armor" is all about shifting from reactive buying ("Oh no, the fridge died!") to proactive planning ("We'll need a new fridge soon, let's look now before prices potentially rise"). It requires keeping your ear to the ground – noticing trends, reading consumer news, maybe even catching manufacturer announcements. It transforms buying necessities from a chore into a strategic move, giving you a sense of control and protecting your wallet from the full force of unpredictable price swings. It's your financial defense strategy, built one smart purchase at a time.

Riding the Wave: Finding Your Flow in the Age of Smart Machines

Forget the creaky old career ladder. These days, building a work-life feels more like navigating a thrilling, sometimes turbulent, river. That's your career curve, and the currents pushing us along? They're powered by technology, especially the smarts of automation and AI. It's not a monster lurking in the future; it's the water we're swimming in right now. The big question isn't if things will change, but how we'll learn the strokes to ride these waves with skill and maybe even a little bit of joy.

Think about this: whispers from global groups like the OECD suggest that by 2030, as many as one in four jobs might need a serious skill remix thanks to tech. Dive into the research, and you'll see countless studies mapping out how automation is weaving itself into the fabric of nearly every industry. This isn't a panic button announcement; it's a friendly, urgent nudge – a call to tune in and prepare for the remix.

But what does this "job shift" really feel like on the ground? Often, it's not about your job title vanishing overnight. It's more like the job description itself is getting a makeover. Imagine the tasks that feel like robotic repetition – the endless data entry, the predictable sorting, the heavy lifting. Automation is getting really good at those, like a tireless assistant taking over the chores.

And here's the beautiful paradox: as machines handle the mundane, it frees us up for the stuff that truly makes us human. Suddenly, there's a bigger craving for your brilliant ideas, your clever problem-solving, your ability to connect with people, your creative spark, and your knack for understanding complex situations. These are the skills that make AI scratch its virtual head, the very things that automation amplifies rather than replaces.

Let's paint a picture. Meet Alex, who used to spend hours buried in spreadsheets and filing. Alex saw the digital tide rising and decided to learn to surf. Maybe through a workshop, an online course, or just tinkering, Alex learned how those automated systems work – maybe even how to guide them or fix them when they hiccup. Alex didn't just dodge obsolescence; Alex leveled up. From doing the routine task, Alex became the conductor, the troubleshooter, the human intelligence behind the automation. That's not just job security; that's career evolution.

This isn't a lone fairy tale:

On the Factory Floor: Workers who once assembled parts by hand are now the tech-savvy guides for robotic arms, shifting from physical repetition to strategic oversight – a true dance between human and machine.

In the Doctor's Office: Radiologists now team up with AI that spots patterns in scans with lightning speed, freeing the doctor's sharp eyes and experienced mind for the complex diagnoses and human element of care.

At the Help Desk: Chatbots field the simple questions, letting human agents dive into the tricky, emotionally charged conversations where empathy and real understanding make all the difference.

So, what's the secret handshake for thriving in this new era? It's not necessarily about becoming a coding guru overnight (though tech skills are undeniably valuable!). It's about nurturing a heartset of curiosity and adaptability. It's about looking at your own work with fresh eyes: What parts feel like they could run on autopilot? What new skills are bubbling up in your field? And where can you learn them – formally or informally?

Embracing your career curve means seeing technological change not as a looming threat, but as a catalyst. It's an invitation to grow, to stretch, to become more versatile, and ultimately, more resilient. It's about finding your unique flow on this ever-changing river, ensuring you're not just keeping afloat, but powerfully steering towards a future full of possibility.

About Author

Azhar ul Haque Sario is a bestselling author and data scientist with a remarkable record of achievement. This Cambridge alumnus brings a wealth of knowledge to his work, holding an MBA, ACCA (Knowledge Level - FTMS College Malaysia), BBA, and several Google certifications, including specializations in Google Data Analytics, Google Digital Marketing & E-commerce, and Google Project Management.

With ten years of business experience, Azhar combines practical expertise with his impressive academic background to craft insightful books. His prolific writing has resulted in an astounding 2810 published titles, earning him the record for the maximum Kindle editions and paperback books published by an individual author in one year, awarded by Asia Books of Records in 2024.

ORCID: https://orcid.org/0009-0004-8629-830X
Azhar.sario@hotmail.co.uk
https://www.linkedin.com/in/azharulhaquesario/

www.ingramcontent.com/pod-product-compliance
Lightning Source LLC
Chambersburg PA
CBHW031349230926
51848CB00002B/453
9783384586018